IoT Beginners Guide Level 1: ESP32, ESP8266, and Arduino Wi-Fi Basics Projects

First Edition
Sarful Hassan

Preface

Who This Book Is For
This book is perfect for **absolute beginners** who want to learn about **IoT (Internet of Things)**. It will help you start making cool projects using **ESP32, ESP8266, and Arduino with Wi-Fi**. If you have little or no experience with electronics or programming, don't worry—this book will guide you step by step.

How This Book Is Organized
The book is divided into **eight chapters**, starting with the basics of **ESP32 and ESP8266** microcontrollers. You'll learn how to use **digital and analog inputs and outputs**, work with **variables, loops**, and **timing functions**, and finally, you'll explore **Wi-Fi-based projects**. At the end of each chapter, you'll find a **simple project** to practice what you've learned.

What Was Left Out
To keep this book easy to follow, some **advanced topics** like deep networking settings or professional IoT platforms are not covered. You can explore those on your own after mastering the basics.

Code Style (About the Code)
The code examples in this book are kept **simple and easy to understand**. You'll see **proper spacing, comments**, and **short, clear lines of code** that show exactly what each step does. The examples use **Micropython**, a popular programming language for microcontrollers.

Micropython Platform Release Notes
The book uses **Micropython** on **version 1.19.x**, which works well with **ESP32 and ESP8266**. Make sure you have an updated version to avoid compatibility issues.

Notes on the First Edition
This is the **first edition**, aimed at helping beginners get started with IoT using **ESP32, ESP8266**, and **Arduino**. Your feedback is welcome to help improve future editions.

Conventions Used in This Book

- **Important terms** and tips are written in bold.
- `Code is shown like this` so you can easily spot it.
- **Numbered steps** are used to make instructions clear.
- Notes and warnings are highlighted so you won't miss them.

Using Code Examples
You're free to **use and change the code examples** for your personal projects. If you want to use the code for **commercial projects**, please get permission.

MechatronicsLAB Online Learning
For more learning resources, visit MechatronicsLAB. You can find **tutorials, courses**, and join a **community of beginners** like you. Contact us at **mechatronicslab@gmail.com** for any questions.

How to Contact Us

- **Email**: mechatronicslab@gmail.com
- **Website**: mechatronicslab.net

Acknowledgments for the First Edition
A big thank you to the **Arduino, ESP32, and ESP8266 communities** and to everyone who has worked on **Micropython**. Your dedication makes learning IoT easy and fun for everyone.

Copyright

Disclaimer
This book is **for educational purposes only**. We are **not responsible** for any problems or damage caused by using the information or code in the book. Always be **careful** when working with electronics.

Chapter-1 Introduction to ESP32

1.Overview of ESP32 and ESP8266

The **ESP32 and ESP8266** are microcontrollers developed by **Espressif Systems**, commonly used in **Internet of Things (IoT)** projects. These microcontrollers are known for their **built-in Wi-Fi** capabilities, which make them highly popular for connecting devices to the internet and creating smart, connected systems. Both are affordable and widely used, but they have different levels of power, features, and applications, making them suitable for different use cases.

- **ESP32**: Designed to be a high-performance microcontroller with dual-core processing, Wi-Fi, and Bluetooth capabilities, the ESP32 is ideal for more advanced IoT projects. It is suitable for applications where more computing power, additional features, and enhanced connectivity are needed.
- **ESP8266**: Known for its low cost and built-in Wi-Fi, the ESP8266 is ideal for simpler IoT projects, particularly for beginners or budget-conscious makers. It's capable of handling basic tasks and is perfect for projects that do not require the higher performance or additional connectivity options found in the ESP32.

Introduction to ESP32

The **ESP32** is a powerful and versatile microcontroller unit (MCU) created by Espressif Systems, specifically designed to enable connected, smart, and interactive devices. The key highlights of the ESP32 are:

- **Dual-Core Processor**: The ESP32 features two Xtensa LX6 processors, each capable of running up to **240 MHz**. This dual-core setup makes it powerful enough for multitasking and managing different operations simultaneously, which is beneficial in many IoT scenarios.
- **Connectivity**: It supports **Wi-Fi** (802.11 b/g/n) and **Bluetooth**, including **Bluetooth Low Energy (BLE)**. This makes the ESP32 versatile, as it can connect to the internet or other devices via Bluetooth.
- **Power Management**: The ESP32 is known for its various **low-power modes**, which makes it ideal for battery-powered

applications. It can operate in **deep sleep mode** with very low power consumption, which is an essential feature for IoT projects that need to last long on a single battery charge.

- **Peripherals and GPIO**: The ESP32 comes with a wide range of **GPIO (General Purpose Input/Output) pins**, which can be used to connect sensors, LEDs, buttons, and other devices. It also has built-in modules like **analog-to-digital converters (ADC)**, **touch sensors**, and a **temperature sensor**.
- **Applications**: It is well-suited for **smart home automation**, **wearables**, **wireless sensors**, and **other advanced IoT projects** that require a high level of connectivity and computation power.

Introduction to ESP8266

The **ESP8266** is an earlier microcontroller model from Espressif Systems, widely popular for its affordability and integrated Wi-Fi. Key characteristics of the ESP8266 are:

- **Single-Core Processor**: The ESP8266 features a **32-bit Tensilica L106 processor**, running at speeds between **80 MHz and 160 MHz**. While it's not as powerful as the ESP32, it is sufficient for less demanding IoT projects, especially those that don't require extensive data processing.
- **Built-in Wi-Fi**: The ESP8266 has a built-in **Wi-Fi module**, making it perfect for connecting small devices to the internet without needing an external Wi-Fi chip. It supports standard Wi-Fi protocols for internet access.
- **Cost-Effectiveness**: The ESP8266 is known for being **highly affordable**, which is why it became popular with hobbyists and makers. It provides a low-cost way to add Wi-Fi capabilities to electronics.
- **GPIO and Connectivity**: It has a limited number of **GPIO pins** compared to the ESP32, which limits the number of sensors and peripherals that can be connected simultaneously. Nevertheless, it supports common communication protocols like **SPI**, **I2C**, and **UART**, making it versatile enough for many smaller projects.
- **Applications**: The ESP8266 is ideal for simple projects such as **smart light switches**, **basic wireless sensors**, and **simple automation devices** where a low-cost solution is needed.

Comparison between ESP32 and ESP8266

To help understand the differences and choose between ESP32 and ESP8266, let's compare their features:

1. **Processing Power**:
    - **ESP32**: Features a **dual-core processor**, running up to **240 MHz**, providing more processing power for demanding applications.
    - **ESP8266**: Has a **single-core processor** running at **80-160 MHz**, sufficient for simple tasks and straightforward IoT projects.
2. **Connectivity**:
    - **ESP32**: Offers both **Wi-Fi** and **Bluetooth (including BLE)** connectivity. This dual connectivity makes it ideal for projects that require a variety of communication options.
    - **ESP8266**: Offers only **Wi-Fi** connectivity, making it great for basic IoT projects that involve internet communication without the need for Bluetooth.
3. **Power Consumption**:
    - **ESP32**: Comes with advanced power-saving features, including multiple power modes (like **deep sleep mode**), which make it suitable for battery-operated projects.
    - **ESP8266**: Also supports power-saving, but it is less efficient than the ESP32, which may affect long-term battery life in some projects.
4. **GPIO and Peripherals**:
    - **ESP32**: Has more **GPIO pins** and a richer set of built-in peripherals, including touch sensors, analog inputs, and a temperature sensor, giving more flexibility for complex projects.
    - **ESP8266**: Has fewer GPIO pins, limiting the number of devices that can be connected, but is still capable of handling basic hardware interfaces and common sensors.
5. **Price**:
    - **ESP8266**: **Cheaper** compared to the ESP32, making it the preferred option for budget projects and for beginners just getting into IoT.
    - **ESP32**: Slightly **more expensive** but worth the cost for projects that require more features and better performance.

6. **Suitability for Projects**:
   - **ESP32**: Best for **advanced IoT projects**, requiring high processing power, Bluetooth connectivity, and multiple sensor inputs. Examples include **smart home automation systems**, **wearable devices**, and **complex sensors**.
   - **ESP8266**: Great for **entry-level and basic IoT projects**, where cost and simplicity are the main factors. It is perfect for **home automation**, such as smart lights and switches, where only Wi-Fi is required.

Pinout and Hardware Layout

Understanding the pinout and hardware layout of microcontrollers like **ESP32** and **ESP8266** is essential for connecting sensors, peripherals, and other electronic components effectively. Both ESP32 and ESP8266 have different sets of pins with specific functions that define their use cases in projects.

ESP32 Pinout Diagram

The **ESP32** microcontroller comes with numerous **GPIO pins** and a variety of other specialized pins that can be used for different purposes. Here's a high-level description of the **ESP32 pinout**:

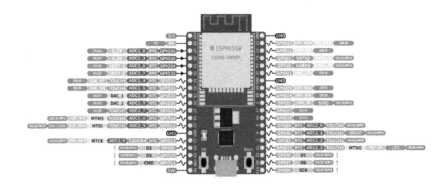

- **GPIO Pins**: The ESP32 typically has **36 GPIO pins** (depending on the variant). These pins can be used as digital inputs or outputs. Many of these pins also have additional functions, such as PWM, ADC, or touch sensors.

- **Power Pins**:
    - **3.3V Pin**: Supplies 3.3 volts of power to the board.
    - **Vin Pin**: This pin is used to power the ESP32 from an external 5V power source.
    - **Ground (GND) Pins**: Connect to the ground of the circuit.
- **Analog Input Pins (ADC)**: The ESP32 has multiple ADC pins that can be used to read analog sensors. There are **18 channels** available, with a resolution of up to **12 bits**.
- **Touch Sensors**: The ESP32 has **capacitive touch pins** (T0 to T9), allowing for touch-based input detection.
- **UART, SPI, I2C, and PWM Pins**: These pins provide communication interfaces to connect peripherals.
    - **UART**: Supports up to 3 UART interfaces for serial communication.
    - **SPI/I2C**: Multiple SPI and I2C pins allow for interfacing with sensors and other devices.
    - **PWM**: Most GPIOs can be used for **PWM** (Pulse Width Modulation), useful for controlling LEDs and motors.
- **Other Special Pins**:
    - **EN Pin**: The **Enable** pin (EN) is used to reset the microcontroller.
    - **Boot Pin (IO0)**: Used to put the ESP32 into **bootloader mode** for uploading firmware.

ESP8266 Pinout Diagram

The **ESP8266** has fewer pins compared to the ESP32, and understanding its pinout is crucial for using it effectively in simpler projects.

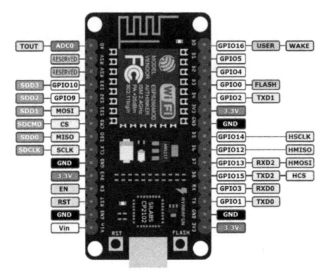

- **GPIO Pins**: The ESP8266 generally has **17 GPIO pins** available (depending on the development board). These pins serve multiple functions and can be configured as digital input or output.
- **Power Pins**:
  - **3.3V Pin**: Supplies power to the ESP8266 (typically operates at 3.3V).
  - **Vin Pin**: Powers the module with an input voltage range of 4.5V to 12V, depending on the board.
  - **Ground (GND) Pins**: Connects to the ground of the circuit.
- **Analog Input Pin (ADC0)**: The ESP8266 has **one analog input pin** (ADC0), which can measure voltages from 0 to 1V.
- **UART, SPI, I2C, and PWM Pins**:
  - **UART**: Supports serial communication for programming and debugging.
  - **SPI/I2C**: Fewer communication options compared to ESP32, but SPI and I2C are still supported for external components.
  - **PWM**: Limited GPIO pins can be configured for PWM, mainly for controlling simple components like LEDs.

- **CH_PD Pin**: The **Chip Power-Down** pin is used to enable or disable the chip.

Pin Functions and Description

Power Pins

- **ESP32 and ESP8266 both have 3.3V and GND pins** for power supply. It's crucial to ensure that the **input voltage** is regulated to prevent damaging the microcontrollers.
- The **Vin pin** can be used to provide external power; however, the voltage requirements for ESP32 and ESP8266 may vary slightly depending on the board.

Input/Output Pins

- Both **ESP32** and **ESP8266** GPIO pins can be configured as **inputs or outputs,** making them versatile for controlling components like LEDs, motors, or reading sensor values.
- **ESP32**: Offers **more GPIO pins** (typically 36), which allows more components to be connected simultaneously.
- **ESP8266**: Offers fewer GPIO pins (usually **17**), which can be a limitation when attempting to connect multiple peripherals.

GPIO Limitations and Considerations

- **ESP32**:
    - Not all GPIO pins are available for general use. Some pins have specific functions (e.g., flash, boot mode) and should be avoided in general-purpose use unless configured correctly.
    - Pins like **GPIO6 to GPIO11** are used for the internal flash and should **not** be used for other purposes.
- **ESP8266**:
    - **GPIO0, GPIO2, and GPIO15**: These pins have special functions during boot mode and should be used carefully to avoid conflicts during power-up.
    - **Limited Number of GPIOs**: With fewer GPIOs, you may need to use **multiplexing** techniques or **GPIO expanders** to connect additional components.

I

nterrupt Capabilities

- **ESP32**: Supports **interrupts** on almost all GPIO pins. This feature is crucial when you need the microcontroller to respond immediately to an event, like a button press.
- **ESP8266**: Interrupts are also supported but are more limited. Care should be taken to avoid using certain pins that may not properly support interrupts.

Analog Input Limitations

- **ESP32**:
  - The ESP32 has **multiple ADC channels** (up to 18), with a 12-bit resolution, which provides more precise analog readings.
  - However, the **ADC** is known to be **non-linear**, and calibration may be required to get accurate results.
- **ESP8266**:
  - The **ESP8266** has only **one ADC pin** (ADC0), and its range is limited to 0-1V, which can be restrictive when trying to read analog signals with higher voltages.
  - A voltage divider may be needed to bring the input voltage within the acceptable range of the ADC.

GPIO Pin Details and Usage for ESP32 and ESP8266

GPIO Pin Number	Pin Type	ESP32	ESP8266	Use
GPIO 0	Digital I/O	Yes	Yes	Boot mode selection, LED control
GPIO 1 (TX)	UART TX	Yes	Yes	Serial communication (data transmission)
GPIO 2	Digital I/O	Yes	Yes	LED control, status indication
GPIO 3 (RX)	UART RX	Yes	Yes	Serial communication (data reception)
GPIO 4	Digital I/O	Yes	Yes	General-purpose tasks, sensors, LEDs
GPIO 5	Digital I/O	Yes	Yes	Motor control, PWM
GPIO 6-11	Flash Memory	No	No	Reserved (do not use)
GPIO 12	Digital I/O	Yes	Yes	General-purpose tasks, output devices
GPIO 13	Digital I/O, PWM	Yes	Yes	LED dimming, motor control

GPIO 14	Digital I/O, PWM	Yes	Yes	PWM for motor or LED, sensor input
GPIO 15	Digital I/O, PWM	Yes	Yes	PWM, sensor or device control
GPIO 16	Digital I/O, Wake	Yes	Yes	Wake from deep sleep, low-power projects
GPIO 17	Digital I/O	Yes	No	General-purpose tasks
GPIO 18	SPI SCK	Yes	No	SPI communication (clock line)
GPIO 19	SPI MISO	Yes	No	SPI communication (data reception)
GPIO 21	I2C SDA	Yes	No	I2C communication (data line)
GPIO 22	I2C SCL	Yes	No	I2C communication (clock line)
GPIO 23	SPI MOSI	Yes	No	SPI communication (data transmission)
GPIO 25-27	Digital I/O, ADC	Yes	No	Reading analog values from sensors
GPIO 32-39	ADC	Yes	No	Analog input (e.g., sensors like LDRs)

Power Supply Requirements:

Voltage Range and Power Consumption:

- **ESP32**: The ESP32 operates within a voltage range of **3.0V to 3.6V**, with an ideal input voltage of **3.3V**. It is capable of drawing a substantial amount of current, especially during Wi-Fi transmission. During peak usage (like Wi-Fi transmission), the ESP32 can consume around **160-240 mA**, while in idle mode, it typically consumes around **20-30 mA**.
- **ESP8266**: The ESP8266 also operates in a voltage range of **3.0V to 3.6V**, typically running at **3.3V**. Its power consumption is slightly lower than that of the ESP32, with peak currents reaching **170 mA** during Wi-Fi transmission. In idle mode, the current draw is roughly **10-20 mA**.

Power Management Hardware: Both ESP32 and ESP8266 have built-in capabilities to manage power consumption effectively:

- **Voltage Regulators**: Most development boards for the ESP32 and ESP8266 (such as NodeMCU or ESP32 DevKit) come with onboard **voltage regulators** that convert higher input voltages (like 5V from USB) to the required **3.3V** for the microcontroller. These voltage regulators ensure that the input power is within the safe operating range.
- **Decoupling Capacitors**: To ensure stable voltage supply and avoid fluctuations during peak power usage, decoupling capacitors are often included on development boards.

Battery Power and USB Power Options:

- **Battery Power**: Both ESP32 and ESP8266 can be powered using batteries, making them ideal for portable projects. Typical battery options include **Li-ion/Li-Po** batteries (3.7V nominal voltage). For battery-powered setups, a voltage regulator is necessary to step down the voltage to **3.3V**. The ESP32 is designed with several power-saving modes, making it suitable for long-term battery-powered applications.
- **USB Power**: Development boards for both ESP32 and ESP8266 generally have a **micro USB port** for powering and programming the microcontroller. The USB power supplies **5V**, which is then regulated down to **3.3V** on the board.

Current Draw During Different States:

Active Mode:

- **ESP32**: In active mode, when all components are running, including Wi-Fi, the ESP32 can consume between **160-240 mA**. This high power draw occurs primarily during transmission and data processing. The dual-core processor adds to the power requirements when both cores are in operation.
- **ESP8266**: In active mode with Wi-Fi enabled, the ESP8266 draws about **150-170 mA**. This is slightly lower compared to the ESP32 due to its simpler architecture and lower processing power.

Sleep Mode:

- **ESP32**: The ESP32 is highly optimized for low-power operation, offering several sleep modes, including **light sleep** and **deep sleep**. In **deep sleep mode**, the ESP32 can reduce its power consumption to around **10 μA**, making it suitable for battery-powered devices where long operational life is required. **Light sleep** typically uses a bit more power, around **1-5 mA**.
- **ESP8266**: The ESP8266 also offers sleep modes, although they are less sophisticated compared to the ESP32. In **deep sleep mode**, the ESP8266 can reduce power consumption to about **20 μA**, which is higher than the ESP32. The wake-up process from deep sleep is relatively slower, which may affect its use in some applications requiring quick responses.

Development Environment and Getting Started

Programming Platforms:

Arduino IDE: The **Arduino IDE** is one of the most beginner-friendly environments for programming both the **ESP32** and **ESP8266**. It provides a simplified interface with numerous examples and libraries that make it easy to get started.

- To use ESP32 or ESP8266 with Arduino IDE, you need to add support by going to **File > Preferences**, then adding the board manager URL for ESP:
  - **ESP32**:
    https://dl.espressif.com/dl/package_esp32_index.json
  - **ESP8266**:
    *http://arduino.esp8266.com/stable/package_esp8266
    com_index.json*
- Once added, you can install the board package via **Tools > Board > Boards Manager** and select the appropriate board for your project.

ESP-IDF (Espressif IoT Development Framework): **ESP-IDF** is the official development framework for the **ESP32** and is more suited for advanced users who want more control over the hardware.

- It provides a comprehensive set of libraries and tools, supporting advanced features such as dual-core operation, Wi-Fi, and Bluetooth configurations.
- Setting up ESP-IDF involves installing the toolchain, Python dependencies, and setting up environment variables. It provides more flexibility and is suitable for professionals working on production-level projects.

MicroPython: **MicroPython** is a popular option for those who prefer scripting over compiled code. It is ideal for rapid prototyping, and both the **ESP32** and **ESP8266** support MicroPython.

- MicroPython can be flashed onto the device, allowing you to write Python scripts to interact with the hardware. It's a great option for beginners who already have some familiarity with Python programming.
- Tools like **Thonny** or **uPyCraft** IDEs make it easy to connect to and program MicroPython on ESP modules.

Required Hardware and Tools:

USB-to-Serial Converter: Most **ESP32** and **ESP8266** development boards, like NodeMCU and ESP32 DevKit, come with a built-in USB-to-serial converter, allowing easy connection to your computer via USB. For standalone modules (e.g., ESP-12 or ESP-01), an external **USB-to-Serial converter** (e.g., **CP2102** or **FTDI232**) is required for flashing and communication.

Power Supply Modules: For reliable operation, a **power supply module** is often needed to provide a stable **3.3V** supply. This can be achieved via:

- **USB Power**: The development boards can be powered through a USB cable.
- **Battery Power**: **Li-ion/Li-Po** batteries are commonly used, especially for portable projects.

Setting Up Development Environment for Multiple OS:

Windows Setup:

1. Install **Arduino IDE** and add ESP32 or ESP8266 board support through the **Boards Manager**.
2. Install the necessary **USB drivers** (e.g., **CP2102** or **CH340** drivers) for Windows to recognize the board.
3. For **ESP-IDF**, download and install the ESP-IDF Tools Installer, which will automatically set up Python, Git, and other dependencies.

macOS Setup:

1. Download and install **Arduino IDE**.
2. Use the macOS **Board Manager URL** to add ESP32 or ESP8266 support.
3. Install **Homebrew** for additional dependencies and install drivers using *brew install*.
4. Set up **ESP-IDF** by following Espressif's installation guide for macOS, which includes setting up Git and Python dependencies.

Linux Setup:

1. Install **Arduino IDE** from the official website and add the required board manager URLs.
2. Linux usually has most USB drivers built-in, but additional permissions might be required to access the serial ports (*/dev/ttyUSB0* or */dev/ttyAMA0*). You may need to add your user to the **dialout** group: *sudo usermod -a -G dialout $USER*
3. Install the **ESP-IDF** by following the official Linux installation guide, which includes installing necessary dependencies via package managers like **apt**.

Basic Troubleshooting for Setup (Driver Issues, Flashing Problems):

Driver Issues:

- If your computer does not recognize the ESP32 or ESP8266, you may need to install drivers for **USB-to-Serial chips** like **CP2102**, **CH340**, or **FTDI**.
- Ensure that the correct COM port is selected in the **Arduino IDE** under **Tools > Port**.

Flashing Problems:

- **Common Errors**: "Failed to connect to ESP32" is a common error when the microcontroller is not in bootloader mode. Press and hold the **BOOT** button while uploading code to put the ESP32 in flashing mode.
- Ensure the **baud rate** is set correctly (usually *115200*).

Flashing Firmware:

Using ESP-Tool to Flash:

- **ESP-Tool** is a command-line utility provided by Espressif for flashing firmware onto ESP32 and ESP8266 devices.
- **Installation**: Install esptool using Python's package manager: *pip install esptool*
- **Usage**: Connect your ESP board and run the following command to erase the flash memory: *esptool.py erase_flash* To flash new firmware: *esptool.py --port COM3 write_flash -z*

0x0000 firmware.bin Replace *COM3* with the appropriate port (e.g., */dev/ttyUSB0* on Linux) and *firmware.bin* with the path to your firmware file.

Troubleshooting Common Issues:

USB Connectivity Problems (Beyond Initial Setup): Even after setting up the initial development environment, you might encounter USB connectivity issues:

- **USB Port Not Recognized**:
    - *Check USB Cable*: Some USB cables are power-only and do not support data transfer. Make sure you are using a **data-capable USB cable**.
    - *Port Selection*: Ensure the correct **COM port** is selected in the **Arduino IDE** under **Tools > Port**.
    - *Reinstall Drivers*: Sometimes, drivers may become corrupted. Reinstalling drivers for **CP2102**, **CH340**, or **FTDI** can help resolve recognition issues.
- **Board Keeps Disconnecting**:
    - *Power Supply Issue*: Ensure that the board is receiving stable power. A poor-quality USB cable or insufficient power from the USB port can cause disconnections. Using a powered USB hub can provide a more stable power supply.
    - *USB Port Overload*: Avoid plugging multiple power-consuming devices into the same USB hub as your ESP board, as this may cause voltage drops, resulting in random disconnections.

Wi-Fi Connectivity Issues:

- **Unable to Connect to Wi-Fi**:
    - *Wrong Credentials*: Double-check the **SSID** and **password**. Simple typos can lead to connection failures.
    - *Wi-Fi Signal Strength*: Place the ESP module closer to the router or access point, and ensure there aren't many obstacles. Use the **WiFi.RSSI()** function in **Arduino IDE** or similar methods to check signal strength.
    - *Channel Overcrowding*: Many Wi-Fi networks on the same channel can cause interference. If possible, change the router's channel to a less crowded one.

- **Intermittent Wi-Fi Disconnection**:
    - *Power Supply Stability*: Ensure a stable power supply, as Wi-Fi transmission draws significant current. Voltage fluctuations can cause the microcontroller to reset or disconnect from Wi-Fi.
    - *Firmware Update*: Older firmware may have issues maintaining a stable Wi-Fi connection. Updating to the latest **ESP32 or ESP8266 firmware** can resolve such issues.

Debugging Tools and Techniques:

- **Serial Monitor**:
    - The **Serial Monitor** in **Arduino IDE** is a fundamental tool for debugging. Use *Serial.print()* statements to understand the flow of your code and identify where errors occur.
- **Logic Analyzers**:
    - For communication issues (such as **I2C** or **SPI**), a **logic analyzer** can help you understand what data is being transmitted and identify where errors might be occurring.
- **ESP-IDF Monitor**:
    - If using **ESP-IDF**, the integrated **ESP-IDF Monitor** provides useful logs and real-time debugging information. It is especially useful for understanding deeper issues like crashes or stack traces.

Best Practices for Using ESP32/ESP8266:

Power Supply Stability:

- Ensure a **reliable 3.3V power supply**. Both ESP32 and ESP8266 can draw spikes of current during Wi-Fi transmissions. If you are using a linear regulator, make sure it can handle at least **500 mA** of current.
- When using battery power, consider a **Li-Po battery** with a **DC-DC buck converter** to ensure stable voltage, as voltage drops can cause unexpected reboots.

Proper GPIO Usage:

- **ESP32**: Not all GPIO pins are available for general use, as some are used internally by the microcontroller (e.g., for flash or boot). Avoid using **GPIO6 to GPIO11** for other purposes, as these are connected to the integrated flash memory.

- **ESP8266**: Special GPIO pins like **GPIO0**, **GPIO2**, and **GPIO15** are involved in the boot process. Ensure proper connections if these pins are used, as incorrect connections can cause the board to not boot correctly.
- Use **current-limiting resistors** (typically **220 ohms to 1k ohms**) when connecting LEDs or other components to GPIO pins to protect both the pins and external components.

Antenna Placement for Wi-Fi:

- **Avoid Obstacles**: The onboard antenna should not be obstructed by metal components, power supplies, or other electronics that could interfere with signal transmission.
- **Distance from Power Sources**: Place the ESP module away from power supplies, as electromagnetic interference can degrade Wi-Fi performance.
- **Proper Orientation**: The onboard PCB antenna is directional. Make sure the module is oriented so that the antenna faces outward for optimal coverage.

Chapter- 2 Arduino Digital I/O

Welcome to this beginner's guide on Arduino Digital I/O, where you'll learn how to use digital pins for input and output operations. By the end of this guide, you'll understand how to control devices like LEDs and read input from buttons or sensors. The guide includes easy-to-follow explanations, sample code, and a real-life project example. Perfect for absolute beginners!

What is Arduino Digital I/O?

Arduino Digital I/O refers to the use of the digital pins on an Arduino board to either **read digital input signals** (e.g., button presses) or **control digital output devices** (e.g., turn an LED on or off). Digital pins can only be in two states: **HIGH** (5V) or **LOW** (0V), corresponding to ON and OFF.

Table of Key Functions for Digital I/O

Serial No.	Topic	Syntax	Simple Example
1	Set a Digital Pin as Output	`pinMode(pin, OUTPUT)`	`pinMode(13, OUTPUT);`
2	Set a Digital Pin as Input	`pinMode(pin, INPUT)`	`pinMode(7, INPUT);`
3	Write a Digital Output (HIGH/LOW)	`digitalWrite(pin, value)`	`digitalWrite(13, HIGH);`
4	Read a Digital Input	`digitalRead(pin)`	`int buttonState = digitalRead(7);`

1. Setting a Digital Pin as Output Using `pinMode(pin, OUTPUT)`

What is `pinMode(pin, OUTPUT)`?

The `pinMode(pin, OUTPUT)` function sets up the specified digital pin to function as an **output** pin, allowing you to control external components such as LEDs, motors, or buzzers.

Use Purpose

- Configures the pin to **send signals**.
- Controls devices like **LEDs** or **motors**.

Arduino Syntax Use

```
pinMode(pin, OUTPUT);
```

Arduino Syntax Explanation

- **pinMode:** This built-in function is used to configure a pin for either input or output. In this case, it sets the pin to output mode.
- **pin:** This parameter is the number of the digital pin being used (e.g., pin 13 for an LED).
- **OUTPUT:** This argument tells the Arduino to set the pin to output mode, allowing it to provide 5V (HIGH) or 0V (LOW) as needed.

Arduino Simple Code Example

```
void setup() {
  pinMode(13, OUTPUT); // Configure pin 13 as an output
}

void loop() {
  digitalWrite(13, HIGH); // Turn the LED on
  delay(1000);            // Wait for 1 second
  digitalWrite(13, LOW);  // Turn the LED off
  delay(1000);            // Wait for 1 second
}
```

2. Setting a Digital Pin as Input Using `pinMode(pin, INPUT)`

What is `pinMode(pin, INPUT)`?

The pinMode(pin, INPUT) function configures the specified digital pin to read the state of an external device, such as a **button** or **sensor**.

Use Purpose

- Detects whether a **button** is pressed or not.
- Reads **digital sensor outputs**.

Arduino Syntax Use

```
pinMode(pin, INPUT);
```

Arduino Syntax Explanation

- **pinMode:** This function sets up a pin for input or output. Here, it configures the pin for input.
- **pin:** The number of the pin to be used for reading input (e.g., pin 7).
- **INPUT:** This argument sets the pin to receive signals.

Arduino Simple Code Example

```
void setup() {
  pinMode(7, INPUT); // Set pin 7 as input
}

void loop() {
  int buttonState = digitalRead(7); // Read the button state
  if (buttonState == HIGH) {
    // Button is pressed
  } else {
    // Button is not pressed
  }
}
```

3. Writing a Digital Output Using digitalWrite(pin, value)

What is digitalWrite(pin, value)?

The `digitalWrite(pin, value)` function controls the output state of a digital pin.

Use Purpose

- Controls the **ON/OFF state** of devices.
- Manages outputs like **LEDs** or **relays**.

Arduino Syntax Use

```
digitalWrite(pin, value);
```

Arduino Syntax Explanation

- **digitalWrite:** Sets the pin to either HIGH (ON) or LOW (OFF).
- **pin:** The pin number where the output is set.
- **value:** Specifies whether to set the pin HIGH (5V) or LOW (0V).

Arduino Simple Code Example

```
void setup() {
  pinMode(13, OUTPUT); // Set pin 13 as output
}

void loop() {
  digitalWrite(13, HIGH); // LED ON
  delay(1000);            // 1-second delay
  digitalWrite(13, LOW);  // LED OFF
  delay(1000);            // 1-second delay
}
```

4. Reading a Digital Input Using `digitalRead(pin)`

What is `digitalRead(pin)`?

The `digitalRead(pin)` function reads the input state of a digital pin, either HIGH or LOW.

Use Purpose

- Checks the **status of a button**.
- Reads input signals from **sensors**.

Arduino Syntax Use

```
int state = digitalRead(pin);
```

Arduino Syntax Explanation

- **digitalRead:** This function reads the state of a specified pin.
- **pin:** The digital pin to read.
- **state:** Stores the read value, either HIGH (5V) or LOW (0V).

Arduino Simple Code Example

```
void setup() {
  pinMode(7, INPUT); // Configure pin 7 as input
}

void loop() {
  int buttonState = digitalRead(7);
  if (buttonState == HIGH) {
    digitalWrite(13, HIGH); // LED ON if button is pressed
  } else {
    digitalWrite(13, LOW); // LED OFF if button is not
pressed
  }
}
```

Complete Real-Life Project: Controlling an LED with a Button

Project Name: Simple LED Button Control
Project Goal:

- Use a button to **toggle the LED state**.
- Show how to read input and control output using **Arduino Digital I/O**.

Project Code

```cpp
#include <Arduino.h>

const int ledPin = 13; // LED at pin 13
const int buttonPin = 7; // Button at pin 7

void setup() {
  pinMode(ledPin, OUTPUT); // Configure LED pin
  pinMode(buttonPin, INPUT); // Configure button pin
}

void loop() {
  int buttonState = digitalRead(buttonPin); // Read button
  if (buttonState == HIGH) {
    digitalWrite(ledPin, HIGH); // LED ON
  } else {
    digitalWrite(ledPin, LOW); // LED OFF
  }
}
```

Save and Run:

1. Copy the code into the **Arduino IDE**.
2. Connect an **LED to pin 13** and a **button to pin 7**.
3. Upload the code to the Arduino.

Check Output:

1. Press the button to turn the **LED ON**.
2. Release the button to turn the **LED OFF**.

Best Practices for Arduino Digital I/O

- **Use Resistors:** Stabilize button states with pull-up or pull-down resistors.
- **Avoid High Currents:** Do not connect heavy loads directly to digital pins.
- **Debounce Buttons:** Use software techniques to reduce false button presses.
- **Delay Management:** Use minimal delays to ensure responsive code.

Chapter-3 Arduino Analog I/O

In this beginner's guide, you will learn the fundamentals of using **Arduino Analog I/O** to read analog signals and generate analog-like output. By the end of this tutorial, you'll know how to read varying sensor values and control devices like LED brightness or motor speed. This guide is perfect for absolute beginners, featuring detailed explanations, syntax usage, and a real-life project example.

What is Arduino Analog I/O?

Arduino Analog I/O involves using the analog pins on the Arduino board to read or write analog signals. Analog inputs read continuous voltage levels (0-5V), providing a range of values, while analog outputs (PWM) simulate varying voltage levels by switching between HIGH and LOW states rapidly.

Key Functions for Analog I/O Operations

Serial No.	Topic	Syntax	Simple Example
1	Read an Analog Input	analogRead(pin)	int sensorValue = analogRead(A0);
2	Write an Analog Output (PWM)	analogWrite(pin, value)	analogWrite(9, 128);

1. Reading an Analog Input Using analogRead(pin)

What is analogRead(pin)?

The analogRead(pin) function reads the voltage level on an analog pin and returns a value between 0 and 1023, representing a voltage range from 0V to 5V.

Use Purpose

- **Read sensor data**, such as temperature or light levels.
- **Monitor variable voltage signals**.

Arduino Syntax Use

```
int sensorValue = analogRead(pin);
```

Arduino Syntax Explanation

- **analogRead:** This function reads the voltage at the specified analog pin and converts it to a digital value.
- **pin:** The analog input pin number. On most Arduino boards, analog pins are labeled as A0, A1, etc.
- **sensorValue:** A variable to store the returned value, ranging from 0 (0V) to 1023 (5V).

Detailed Explanation:

When reading an analog input, the Arduino converts the voltage (0-5V) at the pin into a 10-bit digital value (0-1023). This allows for detecting varying input levels, such as changes in light intensity or temperature.

Arduino Simple Code Example

```
void setup() {
  Serial.begin(9600); // Start serial communication at 9600
baud rate
}

void loop() {
  int sensorValue = analogRead(A0); // Read the value from
analog pin A0
  Serial.println(sensorValue); // Print the sensor value to
the serial monitor
  delay(100); // Wait 100 milliseconds before reading again
}
```

2. Writing an Analog Output Using analogWrite(pin, value)

What is analogWrite(pin, value)?

The analogWrite(pin, value) function generates a Pulse Width Modulation (PWM) signal to simulate an analog output.

Use Purpose

- **Control the brightness of an LED**.
- **Adjust motor speed**.
- **Generate analog-like output signals**.

Arduino Syntax Use

```
analogWrite(pin, value);
```

Arduino Syntax Explanation

- **analogWrite:** This function sets the output to a specific PWM value.
- **pin:** The digital pin used for PWM output. On most Arduino boards, these pins are marked with a ~ symbol (e.g., 3, 5, 6, 9, 10, 11).
- **value:** A number between 0 and 255 that controls the duty cycle of the PWM signal. A value of 0 sets the output to 0V, while 255 sets it to 5V.

Detailed Explanation:

PWM simulates varying voltage levels by switching the pin between HIGH and LOW states at a high frequency. The ratio between the HIGH time and the LOW time (duty cycle) determines the effective output voltage. For example, a PWM value of 128 generates a signal that is 50% HIGH and 50% LOW, simulating an output of 2.5V.

Arduino Simple Code Example

```
void setup() {
  pinMode(9, OUTPUT); // Set pin 9 as an output for PWM
}

void loop() {
  analogWrite(9, 128); // Set PWM signal with 50% duty cycle
  delay(1000);          // Wait for 1 second
  analogWrite(9, 255); // Set PWM signal to maximum (100%
duty cycle)
```

```
  delay(1000);              // Wait for 1 second
}
```

Complete Real-Life Project: Controlling LED Brightness with a Potentiometer

Project Name: LED Brightness Control with a Potentiometer
Project Goal:

- Use a **potentiometer** to control the brightness of an LED.
- Demonstrate reading an **analog input** and writing an **analog output**.

Project Code

```
#include <Arduino.h>

const int potPin = A0; // Potentiometer connected to analog
pin A0
const int ledPin = 9;  // LED connected to PWM pin 9

void setup() {
  pinMode(ledPin, OUTPUT); // Set the LED pin as output
}

void loop() {
  int potValue = analogRead(potPin); // Read potentiometer
value (0-1023)
  int ledBrightness = map(potValue, 0, 1023, 0, 255); // Map
the value to 0-255
  analogWrite(ledPin, ledBrightness); // Set LED brightness
  delay(10); // Small delay to stabilize the reading
}
```

Save and Run:

1. **Open Arduino IDE** and create a new sketch.
2. **Copy the code** above into the sketch.
3. **Connect a potentiometer to analog pin A0** and an **LED to PWM pin 9**.
4. **Upload the code** to your Arduino board.

Check Output:

1. **Turn the potentiometer** to see the LED brightness change accordingly.
2. **Observe the LED** getting brighter as you increase the potentiometer value and dimmer as you decrease it.

Best Practices for Arduino Analog I/O

- **Filter Noisy Signals:** Use capacitors or software filtering techniques to stabilize analog readings.
- **Avoid Direct Connection to High-Current Devices:** Use transistors or MOSFETs to control motors or high-power LEDs.
- **Calibrate Sensor Readings:** Map sensor input values to meaningful ranges using the map () function.
- **Smooth Analog Output:** Implement software-based smoothing techniques to make outputs smoother.

Chapter-4 Data Types and Variables in Arduino

This beginner-friendly guide explains the fundamentals of **Data Types and Variables in Arduino** programming. You will learn about different data types used to store various kinds of data, how to declare variables, and some best practices for using them effectively. This guide is structured to help absolute beginners get started with Arduino programming, featuring clear explanations and practical examples.

What Are Data Types and Variables in Arduino?

Data Types in Arduino define the kind of data a variable can hold, such as integers, floating-point numbers, or characters. **Variables** are named storage locations in memory that hold data and can be modified during the program execution. Understanding how to use data types and variables is essential for storing values and performing calculations in Arduino programming.

Common Data Types in Arduino

Serial No.	Data Type	Description	Range	Example Usage
1	int	Stores integer values	-32,768 to 32,767	int count = 10;
2	float	Stores floating-point numbers	±3.4028235E+38 (6-7 decimal digits)	float temperature = 23.5;
3	char	Stores a single character	-128 to 127 (ASCII values)	char letter = 'A';
4	boolean	Stores true or false values	true (1) or false (0)	boolean isOn = true;

5	unsigned int	Stores only positive integer values	0 to 65,535	unsigned int distance = 1000;

1. Using `int` to Store Integer Values

What is `int`?

The `int` data type is used to store whole numbers, both positive and negative, without decimal points. It is one of the most commonly used data types for counting or storing small numerical values in Arduino.

Use Purpose

- **Count iterations in loops.**
- **Store sensor readings** (e.g., temperature, light intensity).

Syntax and Example Usage

```
int count = 10;
```

Explanation

- **int:** Specifies the data type.
- **count:** The name of the variable.
- **10:** The initial value assigned to the variable.

2. Using `float` to Store Decimal Values

What is `float`?

The `float` data type is used to store numbers with decimal points. It is commonly used for **storing measurements** or **calculating mathematical operations** that require precision.

Use Purpose

- **Store sensor values** that have decimal points (e.g., temperature with decimal).

- **Perform calculations** that require floating-point precision.

Syntax and Example Usage

```
float temperature = 23.5;
```

Explanation

- **float:** Indicates a floating-point data type.
- **temperature:** The name of the variable.
- **23.5:** The initial value assigned to the variable.

3. Using char to Store Single Characters

What is char?

The char data type is used to store a single character, such as a letter, digit, or symbol. In Arduino, it can also be used to **store ASCII values**.

Use Purpose

- **Store a single letter** or **symbol** for text-based processing.
- **Work with characters** for **serial communication**.

Syntax and Example Usage

```
char letter = 'A';
```

Explanation

- **char:** Represents the character data type.
- **letter:** The variable name.
- **'A':** The character value assigned to the variable (enclosed in single quotes).

4. Using `boolean` to Store True or False Values

What is `boolean`?

The `boolean` data type is used to represent two states: `true` (1) or `false` (0). It is commonly used for **decision-making** in conditional statements.

Use Purpose

- **Control conditional statements** (e.g., if-else conditions).
- **Track the state** of a device (e.g., is a light on or off?).

Syntax and Example Usage

```
boolean isOn = true; // Declaring a boolean variable named 'isOn' with the value true
```

Explanation

- **boolean:** Defines the data type as a boolean.
- **isOn:** The name of the variable.
- **true:** The initial value (can be true or false).

5. Using `unsigned int` for Positive Integer Values

What is `unsigned int`?

The `unsigned int` data type is used to store **positive integer values only**. It extends the range of `int` by only allowing non-negative numbers.

Use Purpose

- **Measure distances** or **store time intervals**.
- **Count without the possibility of negative values**.

Syntax and Example Usage

```
unsigned int distance = 1000; // Declaring an unsigned integer variable named 'distance' with a value of 1000
```

Explanation

- **unsigned int:** Represents a data type that can only hold positive values.
- **distance:** The name of the variable.
- **1000:** The initial value assigned to the variable.

Declaring and Using Variables in Arduino

Syntax for Declaring a Variable

```
dataType variableName = initialValue;
```

Explanation

- **dataType:** The type of data (e.g., int, float, char, boolean).
- **variableName:** The name used to identify the variable.
- **initialValue:** The value assigned at the time of declaration (optional).

Example

```
int ledPin = 13; // Declare an integer variable to store the pin number for an LED
```

Real-Life Project: Controlling an LED Based on Temperature

Project Name: LED Control Based on Temperature
Project Goal:

- **Read the temperature** using a sensor.
- **Control an LED** based on the temperature value.

Project Code

```
#include <Arduino.h>

const int ledPin = 13; // LED connected to digital pin 13
const int tempPin = A0; // Temperature sensor connected to analog pin A0
float temperature; // Variable to store temperature value
```

```
void setup() {
  pinMode(ledPin, OUTPUT); // Set LED pin as output
  Serial.begin(9600); // Start serial communication
}

void loop() {
  int sensorValue = analogRead(tempPin); // Read the
temperature sensor value
  temperature = (sensorValue * 5.0 / 1023.0) * 100.0; //
Convert to temperature in Celsius

  Serial.print("Temperature: ");
  Serial.println(temperature); // Print temperature to
serial monitor

  if (temperature > 30.0) { // If temperature is greater
than 30 degrees
    digitalWrite(ledPin, HIGH); // Turn on LED
  } else {
    digitalWrite(ledPin, LOW); // Turn off LED
  }

  delay(1000); // Wait for 1 second before repeating
}
```

Save and Run:

1. **Copy the code** into a new Arduino sketch.
2. **Connect a temperature sensor to A0** and an **LED to pin 13**.
3. **Upload the code** to your Arduino board.

Check Output:

1. **Monitor the temperature** readings on the serial monitor.
2. **Observe the LED** turning on if the temperature is above 30°C and turning off otherwise.

Best Practices for Using Data Types and Variables

- **Use Descriptive Variable Names:** Make the code easier to understand.
- **Choose the Appropriate Data Type:** Use smaller data types for efficient memory usage.
- **Initialize Variables:** Always initialize variables to avoid unexpected behavior.
- **Avoid Global Variables:** Use local variables within functions for better memory management.

Chapter-5 Arduino Operator

This guide covers the basics of **Arduino Operators**, which are used for performing operations on variables and values in programming. You'll learn about different types of operators, including arithmetic, comparison, logical, and assignment operators, with easy-to-understand explanations and examples. This guide is designed to help absolute beginners understand how to use operators in Arduino programming.

What Are Operators in Arduino?

Operators in Arduino programming are symbols that perform operations on variables and values. They help in **manipulating data**, **performing calculations**, and **making decisions** within the code. Common operator types include arithmetic, comparison, logical, and assignment operators.

Common Types of Operators in Arduino

Seria l No.	Operator Type	Operator s Used	Description	Exampl e Usage
1	Arithmetic Operators	+, −, *, /, %	Perform basic mathematic al operations	int sum = a + b;
2	Comparison Operators	==, !=, <, >, <=, >=	Compare two values and return true or false	if (a == b)
3	Logical Operators	&&, `		, !
4	Assignment Operators	=, +=, −=, *=, /=, %=	Assign values to variables	a += 5;
5	Increment/Decreme nt	++, −−	Increase or decrease the value of a variable by 1	a++; or b−−;

1. Arithmetic Operators in Arduino

What Are Arithmetic Operators?

Arithmetic operators perform **basic mathematical operations** such as addition, subtraction, multiplication, division, and modulo.

Common Arithmetic Operators

Operator	Description	Example
+	Adds two values	`int sum = a + b;`
−	Subtracts one value from another	`int diff = a - b;`
*	Multiplies two values	`int product = a * b;`
/	Divides one value by another	`int quotient = a / b;`
%	Returns the remainder of a division	`int remainder = a % b;`

Syntax and Example Usage

```
int a = 10;
int b = 3;
int sum = a + b; // Adds a and b, resulting in 13
int diff = a - b; // Subtracts b from a, resulting in 7
int product = a * b; // Multiplies a and b, resulting in 30
int quotient = a / b; // Divides a by b, resulting in 3
int remainder = a % b; // Calculates the remainder,
resulting in 1
```

2. Comparison Operators in Arduino

What Are Comparison Operators?

Comparison operators compare **two values** and return a `true` or `false` result. They are often used in **conditional statements** like `if` statements to **make decisions** in the program.

Common Comparison Operators

Operator	Description	Example
==	Checks if two values are equal	`if (a == b)`
!=	Checks if two values are not equal	`if (a != b)`
<	Checks if one value is less than another	`if (a < b)`
>	Checks if one value is greater than another	`if (a > b)`
<=	Checks if one value is less than or equal to another	`if (a <= b)`
>=	Checks if one value is greater than or equal to another	`if (a >= b)`

Syntax and Example Usage

```
int a = 5;
int b = 10;

if (a < b) {
  // This code will execute because a is less than b
  Serial.println("a is less than b");
}
```

3. Logical Operators in Arduino

What Are Logical Operators?

Logical operators are used to **combine multiple conditions** in a conditional statement. They help **evaluate complex conditions** by combining two or more comparisons.

Common Logical Operators

Operator	Description	Example
&&	Logical AND - returns true if both conditions are true	if (a > b && c < d)
!	Logical NOT - inverts the truth value of the condition	if (!(a > b))

Syntax and Example Usage

```
int a = 5;
int b = 10;
int c = 15;

if (a < b && c > b) {
  // Both conditions are true, so this code will execute
  Serial.println("Both conditions are true");
}
```

4. Assignment Operators in Arduino

What Are Assignment Operators?

Assignment operators are used to **assign values to variables**. They can also perform **arithmetic operations** and **assign the result** in a single step.

Common Assignment Operators

Operator	Description	Example
=	Assigns a value to a variable	a = 5;
+=	Adds a value to a variable and assigns the result	a += 5;
-=	Subtracts a value from a variable and assigns the result	a -= 5;
*=	Multiplies a variable by a value and assigns the result	a *= 5;
/=	Divides a variable by a value and assigns the result	a /= 5;
%=	Finds the remainder of a variable divided by a value and assigns the result	a %= 5;

Syntax and Example Usage

```
int a = 10;
a += 5; // Equivalent to a = a + 5, so a becomes 15
a -= 3; // Equivalent to a = a - 3, so a becomes 12
a *= 2; // Equivalent to a = a * 2, so a becomes 24
a /= 4; // Equivalent to a = a / 4, so a becomes 6
a %= 2; // Equivalent to a = a % 2, so a becomes 0
```

5. Increment and Decrement Operators

What Are Increment and Decrement Operators?

Increment and decrement operators are used to **increase or decrease the value of a variable by 1**. They are often used in **loops** for counting.

Common Increment/Decrement Operators

Operator	Description	Example
++	Increases the value of a variable by 1	a++;
--	Decreases the value of a variable by 1	a--;

Syntax and Example Usage

```
int count = 0;
count++; // Increases count by 1, making it 1
count--; // Decreases count by 1, making it 0
```

Real-Life Project: LED Blink Control with Operators

Project Name: LED Blink Control Based on Arithmetic and Comparison Operators
Project Goal:

- **Control the blink rate of an LED** based on a value calculated using arithmetic operators.
- **Use comparison operators** to change the blink rate.

Project Code

```
#include <Arduino.h>

const int ledPin = 13; // LED connected to digital pin 13
int blinkRate = 500; // Initial blink rate in milliseconds

void setup() {
```

```
  pinMode(ledPin, OUTPUT); // Set the LED pin as output
  Serial.begin(9600); // Start serial communication
}

void loop() {
  blinkRate += 100; // Increase blink rate by 100ms every
loop
  if (blinkRate > 1000) {
    blinkRate = 200; // Reset blink rate if it exceeds
1000ms
  }

  // Blink the LED
  digitalWrite(ledPin, HIGH); // Turn the LED on
  delay(blinkRate); // Wait for the current blink rate
  digitalWrite(ledPin, LOW); // Turn the LED off
  delay(blinkRate); // Wait for the current blink rate

  Serial.print("Current Blink Rate: ");
  Serial.println(blinkRate); // Print the current blink rate
to the serial monitor
}
```

Save and Run:

1. **Copy the code** into a new Arduino sketch.
2. **Connect an LED to pin 13**.
3. **Upload the code** to your Arduino board.

Check Output:

1. **Observe the LED blink** at varying rates as the blink rate changes based on the arithmetic and comparison operations.
2. **Monitor the serial output** to see the current blink rate.

Best Practices for Using Operators in Arduino

- **Use Parentheses for Clarity:** When combining multiple operators in a single statement, use parentheses to make the order of operations clear.

- **Avoid Division by Zero:** Always check values before performing division.
- **Use Increment/Decrement Operators in Loops:** For counting in loops, use ++ or -- to simplify code.
- **Combine Assignment with Arithmetic:** Use compound assignment operators like += or *= for concise code.

Chapter-6 Control Structures in Arduino

This guide explains **Control Structures in Arduino**, which are used to manage the flow of a program by making decisions, repeating code, or breaking out of loops. Understanding these structures is essential for writing effective and flexible code. This beginner-friendly guide covers the most common control structures, including if, else, for, while, and switch statements, with simple examples to help you get started.

What Are Control Structures in Arduino?

Control structures in Arduino are programming elements that **control the flow of execution**. They determine how and when parts of the code are executed based on conditions or iterations. Common control structures include **conditional statements**, **loops**, and **switch-case statements**.

Common Types of Control Structures in Arduino

Serial No.	Control Structure	Description	Example Usage
1	if and else	Make decisions based on conditions	if (a > b)
2	for loop	Repeat code a specified number of times	for (int i = 0; i < 10; i++)
3	while loop	Repeat code while a condition is true	while (a < 10)
4	do-while loop	Repeat code at least once, then check the condition	do { ... } while (condition);
5	switch-case	Choose from multiple cases based on a variable's value	switch (choice)

1. Using if and else Statements

What Are if and else?

The if and else statements allow the program to make **decisions based on conditions**. The if statement checks whether a condition is true and executes the corresponding block of code. The else statement runs if the if condition is false.

Use Purpose

- **Execute code only when certain conditions are met**.
- **Make decisions** in the program based on sensor values or user input.

Syntax and Example Usage

```
int temperature = 25;
```

```
if (temperature > 30) {
  // Code to execute if temperature is above 30
  Serial.println("It's too hot!");
} else {
  // Code to execute if temperature is 30 or below
  Serial.println("Temperature is normal.");
}
```

Explanation

- **if:** Checks if the condition (temperature > 30) is true.
- **else:** Executes if the if condition is false.

2. Using for Loops

What Is a for Loop?

A for loop allows you to **repeat a block of code a specific number of times**. It is commonly used for **iterating over arrays** or **counting up or down**.

Use Purpose

- **Repeat code multiple times** with a defined start and end.
- **Iterate through arrays** or perform repeated tasks.

Syntax and Example Usage
```
for (int i = 0; i < 5; i++) {
  // This code will execute 5 times
  Serial.print("Loop iteration: ");
  Serial.println(i);
}
```

Explanation

- int i = 0: Initializes the loop variable i.
- i < 5: Sets the condition for the loop to continue.
- i++: Increments the loop variable after each iteration.

3. Using while Loops

What Is a while Loop?

A while loop repeats a block of code **as long as a specified condition is true**. The condition is checked before each iteration.

Use Purpose

- **Execute code repeatedly** until a certain condition is met.
- **Monitor sensors** continuously in a program.

Syntax and Example Usage

```
int count = 0;

while (count < 3) {
  // This code will execute while count is less than 3
  Serial.print("Count is: ");
  Serial.println(count);
  count++;
}
```

Explanation

- **while (count < 3):** The loop continues as long as the condition is true.
- **count++:** Increments the variable count after each loop iteration.

4. Using do-while Loops

What Is a do-while Loop?

A do-while loop is similar to a while loop, but the code inside the loop **executes at least once**, regardless of the condition.

Use Purpose

- **Execute code at least once**, even if the condition is initially false.
- **Perform tasks before checking a condition**.

Syntax and Example Usage

```
int x = 0;
```

```
do {
  // This code will execute at least once
  Serial.println("This will print at least once.");
  x++;
} while (x < 3);
```

Explanation

- **do { ... } while (x < 3):** The code block inside the do executes first, then the condition is checked.

5. Using switch-case Statements

What Is a switch-case Statement?

A switch-case statement allows the program to **select from multiple options** based on the value of a variable. It's an alternative to using multiple if-else statements.

Use Purpose

- **Execute different code blocks** based on the value of a variable.
- **Handle multiple cases** where a variable can have distinct values.

Syntax and Example Usage

```
int mode = 2;

switch (mode) {
  case 1:
    Serial.println("Mode 1 selected.");
    break;
  case 2:
    Serial.println("Mode 2 selected.");
    break;
  default:
    Serial.println("Invalid mode.");
    break;
}
```

Explanation

- **switch (mode)**: The variable mode is evaluated.
- **case 1, case 2**: Executes different code blocks based on the value of mode.
- **default**: Executes if none of the cases match.

Real-Life Project: Controlling an LED with Multiple Modes

Project Name: LED Mode Control Based on User Input
Project Goal:

- **Control the LED state** using a switch-case statement.
- **Change the LED behavior** based on user-defined modes.

Project Code

```
#include <Arduino.h>

const int ledPin = 13; // LED connected to digital pin 13
int mode = 0; // Variable to store the selected mode

void setup() {
  pinMode(ledPin, OUTPUT); // Set the LED pin as output
  Serial.begin(9600); // Start serial communication
  Serial.println("Enter a mode (1, 2, or 3):");
}

void loop() {
  // Check if user has entered a mode through the serial
monitor
  if (Serial.available() > 0) {
    mode = Serial.parseInt(); // Read the mode from the
serial monitor

    // Use a switch-case statement to control the LED based
on the mode
    switch (mode) {
      case 1:
```

```
      digitalWrite(ledPin, HIGH); // Turn on LED
      Serial.println("LED is ON.");
      break;
    case 2:
      digitalWrite(ledPin, LOW); // Turn off LED
      Serial.println("LED is OFF.");
      break;
    case 3:
      for (int i = 0; i < 3; i++) { // Blink the LED 3
times
          digitalWrite(ledPin, HIGH);
          delay(500);
          digitalWrite(ledPin, LOW);
          delay(500);
      }
      Serial.println("LED blinked 3 times.");
      break;
    default:
      Serial.println("Invalid mode. Please enter 1, 2, or
3.");
      break;
    }
    Serial.println("Enter a new mode (1, 2, or 3):");
  }
}
```

Save and Run:

1. **Copy the code** into a new Arduino sketch.
2. **Connect an LED to pin 13**.
3. **Upload the code** to your Arduino board.

Check Output:

1. **Open the serial monitor** and enter a mode (1, 2, or 3).
2. **Observe the LED behavior** based on the selected mode.
3. **Enter different modes** to change the LED's operation.

Best Practices for Using Control Structures in Arduino

- **Use Proper Indentation:** Make code easier to read by indenting nested control structures.
- **Break Out of Loops When Needed:** Use the break statement to exit a loop early if required.
- **Avoid Infinite Loops:** Ensure that while or do-while loops have an exit condition.
- **Use Switch-Case for Multiple Choices:** When handling multiple options, switch-case is clearer and more efficient than using many if-else statements.

Chapter-7 Timing and Delays in Arduino

This guide covers the basics of **Timing and Delays in Arduino**, explaining how to manage time-related tasks in your programs. Timing functions help you create delays, measure elapsed time, and schedule events, which are essential for tasks like blinking LEDs, controlling motors, or reading sensor data at regular intervals. This beginner-friendly guide includes detailed explanations and examples to help you get started with timing in Arduino programming.

What Are Timing and Delays in Arduino?

Timing and delays in Arduino are used to control when code executes. They allow you to **pause program execution**, **measure time intervals**, and **schedule tasks**. Common timing functions in Arduino include delay(), millis(), and micros().

Common Timing Functions in Arduino

Serial No.	Function	Description	Example Usage
1	delay ()	Pauses the program for a specified number of milliseconds	delay (1000)
2	millis ()	Returns the number of milliseconds since the program started	unsigned long time = millis ()
3	micros ()	Returns the number of microseconds since the program started	unsigned long time = micros ()
4	delayMicroseconds ()	Pauses the program for a specified number of microseconds	delayMicroseconds (100)

1. Using delay () to Pause Program Execution

What is delay () ?

The delay () function pauses the execution of the program for a specified number of milliseconds. It is a simple way to create delays, often used for **blinking LEDs** or **controlling the timing of events**.

Use Purpose

- **Pause the program** for a specific duration.
- **Create timed intervals** for tasks like blinking an LED.

Syntax and Example Usage

delay(1000); // Pauses the program for 1000 milliseconds (1 second)

Explanation

- The value inside delay() specifies the number of milliseconds to pause the program. For example, delay(1000) pauses for 1 second.

Arduino Simple Code Example

```
void setup() {
  pinMode(13, OUTPUT); // Set pin 13 as an output
}

void loop() {
  digitalWrite(13, HIGH); // Turn the LED on
  delay(1000);            // Wait for 1 second
  digitalWrite(13, LOW);  // Turn the LED off
  delay(1000);            // Wait for 1 second
}
```

2. Using millis() for Measuring Time

What is millis()?

The millis() function returns the number of **milliseconds** that have passed since the program started running. It is useful for **measuring elapsed time** or **scheduling tasks without blocking the program**.

Use Purpose

- **Track elapsed time** in your program.
- **Schedule non-blocking tasks**.

Syntax and Example Usage

```
unsigned long currentTime = millis(); // Stores the number
of milliseconds since the program started
```

Explanation

- millis() returns an **unsigned long** integer, which represents the number of milliseconds since the Arduino started running the current program.

Arduino Simple Code Example

```
unsigned long previousTime = 0;
const long interval = 1000; // Interval of 1 second

void setup() {
  pinMode(13, OUTPUT); // Set pin 13 as an output
}

void loop() {
  unsigned long currentTime = millis(); // Get the current
time

  if (currentTime - previousTime >= interval) {
    previousTime = currentTime; // Update the previous time
    digitalWrite(13, !digitalRead(13)); // Toggle the LED
  }
}
```

3. Using micros() for Microsecond Precision Timing

What is micros()?

The micros() function returns the number of **microseconds** that have passed since the program started. It is useful for tasks that require **higher precision timing**, such as generating pulses or measuring very short intervals.

Use Purpose

- **Measure very short time intervals**.

- **Generate precise pulses** for components like ultrasonic sensors.

Syntax and Example Usage

```
unsigned long currentTime = micros(); // Stores the number
of microseconds since the program started
```

Explanation

- `micros()` returns an **unsigned long** integer, representing the number of microseconds elapsed since the program started. It can be used for tasks that require timing precision in microseconds.

Arduino Simple Code Example

```
unsigned long startTime;

void setup() {
  Serial.begin(9600); // Start serial communication
  startTime = micros(); // Record the start time
}

void loop() {
  unsigned long elapsedTime = micros() - startTime; //
Calculate elapsed time
  Serial.println(elapsedTime); // Print the elapsed time in
microseconds
  delay(1000); // Wait for 1 second before repeating
}
```

4. Using delayMicroseconds() for Short Delays

What is delayMicroseconds()?

The delayMicroseconds() function pauses the program for a specified number of **microseconds**. It is used for tasks that require very short, precise delays, such as **bit-banging protocols**.

Use Purpose

- **Create very short delays** with microsecond precision.
- **Generate signals** with specific timing requirements.

Syntax and Example Usage

```
delayMicroseconds(100); // Pauses the program for 100
microseconds
```

Explanation

- The value inside delayMicroseconds() specifies the number of microseconds to pause the program. It is more precise than delay() for short durations.

Arduino Simple Code Example

```
void setup() {
  pinMode(13, OUTPUT); // Set pin 13 as an output
}

void loop() {
  digitalWrite(13, HIGH); // Turn the LED on
  delayMicroseconds(500); // Wait for 500 microseconds
  digitalWrite(13, LOW);  // Turn the LED off
  delayMicroseconds(500); // Wait for 500 microseconds
}
```

Real-Life Project: Blinking an LED Without Using delay()

Project Name: LED Blinking with millis() Timing
Project Goal:

- **Blink an LED at regular intervals** without using the delay() function.
- **Demonstrate how to use millis()** for non-blocking timing.

Project Code

```
#include <Arduino.h>

const int ledPin = 13; // LED connected to digital pin 13
```

```
unsigned long previousMillis = 0; // Stores the last time
the LED was updated
const long interval = 1000; // Interval for blinking the LED
(1 second)

void setup() {
  pinMode(ledPin, OUTPUT); // Set the LED pin as output
}

void loop() {
  unsigned long currentMillis = millis(); // Get the current
time

  // Check if the interval has elapsed
  if (currentMillis - previousMillis >= interval) {
    previousMillis = currentMillis; // Save the last time
the LED was toggled
    digitalWrite(ledPin, !digitalRead(ledPin)); // Toggle
the LED state
  }
}
```

Save and Run:

1. **Copy the code** into a new Arduino sketch.
2. **Connect an LED to pin 13**.
3. **Upload the code** to your Arduino board.

Check Output:

1. **Observe the LED blinking** at 1-second intervals.
2. **Note that the program remains responsive**, as the millis() function allows non-blocking timing.

Best Practices for Using Timing and Delays in Arduino

- **Use millis() for Non-Blocking Delays:** Avoid using delay() in time-sensitive applications where other tasks need to run concurrently.

- **Keep Track of Unsigned Long Values:** When using millis() or micros(), always store the values in **unsigned long** variables to avoid overflow issues.
- **Limit the Use of delay() for Short Delays:** Reserve delay() for simple tasks or debugging. For more complex timing, use millis().
- **Avoid Long Delays:** Long delays can make your program unresponsive. Use non-blocking techniques to improve performance.

Get started IOT

Chapter-8 IoT with ESP32 Wifi

8.1.Station Mode (STA) on ESP32

This chapter covers how to use **Station Mode (STA) on ESP32** to connect to a Wi-Fi network. In Station Mode, the ESP32 functions as a client, allowing it to connect to an existing Wi-Fi network and interact with the internet or other devices on the network. We will explore essential functions such as connecting to Wi-Fi, checking the connection status, disconnecting, retrieving the local IP address, and more. The guide concludes with a simple real-life project demonstrating practical use.

Syntax Table for Station Mode Functions

Serial No.	Topic	Syntax	Simple Example
1	**Connect to Wi-Fi**	WiFi.begin(ssid, password)	WiFi.begin("MySSID", "MyPassword");
2	**Check Connection Status**	WiFi.status()	if (WiFi.status() == WL_CONNECTED) { /* ... */ }
3	**Disconnect from Wi-Fi**	WiFi.disconnect()	WiFi.disconnect();
4	**Get Local IP Address**	WiFi.localIP()	IPAddress ip = WiFi.localIP();

5	**Reconnect to Wi-Fi**	WiFi.reconnect()	WiFi.reconnect();
6	**Check if Connected**	WiFi.isConnected()	if (WiFi.isConnected()) { /* ... */ }
7	**Scan for Networks**	WiFi.scanNetworks()	int n = WiFi.scanNetworks();

This table provides a quick reference for essential functions in **Station Mode on ESP32**, enabling basic Wi-Fi management.

---

1. Connecting to Wi-Fi Using WiFi.begin(ssid, password)

What is WiFi.begin(ssid, password)?

WiFi.begin(ssid, password) is the function used to connect the ESP32 to a Wi-Fi network in Station Mode. It requires the network's SSID (name) and password to initiate the connection.

Use Purpose

This function is used to:

- **Connect the ESP32 to a Wi-Fi network** for internet access.
- **Enable communication with other network devices** or online services.
- **Allow remote data monitoring and transmission.**

Arduino Syntax Use
WiFi.begin(ssid, password);

Arduino Syntax Explanation

1. **WiFi**: Refers to the built-in Wi-Fi library for the ESP32. It provides a set of functions for managing Wi-Fi connections, configuring network parameters, and retrieving network information.
2. **begin()**: This function initiates the connection process by attempting to connect the ESP32 to a Wi-Fi network using the provided SSID and password.
   o **What it does**: begin() starts the connection process in Station Mode (STA), where the ESP32 acts as a client on an existing Wi-Fi network. The function attempts to authenticate with the Wi-Fi router using the given credentials.
3. **ssid**: This parameter specifies the Service Set Identifier (SSID), which is the name of the Wi-Fi network you want the ESP32 to connect to.
   o **Data Type**: const char* (a string in C++)
   o **Purpose**: Specifies which Wi-Fi network to join. For example, if your Wi-Fi network is named "HomeWiFi," you would pass "HomeWiFi" as the ssid.
4. **password**: This parameter specifies the password required to access the Wi-Fi network.
   o **Data Type**: const char* (a string in C++)
   o **Purpose**: Used for authenticating with the Wi-Fi network. It must match the password set on the Wi-Fi router. For example, if your password is "SecurePassword123," you would pass "SecurePassword123" as the password.
5. **Return Value**: The function itself does not return a value directly. The success or failure of the connection is determined by checking the connection status using WiFi.status() after calling begin().

Arduino Simple Code Example

```
#include <WiFi.h>

// Wi-Fi credentials
const char* ssid = "Your_SSID";        // Replace with
your network's SSID
```

```
const char* password = "Your_PASSWORD";   // Replace with
your network's password

void setup() {
  Serial.begin(115200);
  WiFi.begin(ssid, password);
  Serial.print("Connecting to Wi-Fi");

  // Wait for the connection to establish
  while (WiFi.status() != WL_CONNECTED) {
    delay(500);
    Serial.print(".");
  }

  Serial.println("\nConnected to Wi-Fi!");
}

void loop() {
  // Main code here
}
```

Notes

- Make sure the ESP32 is within the range of the Wi-Fi network.
- The SSID and password must match exactly, including case sensitivity.

Warnings

- **Hardcoding Wi-Fi credentials** can be a security risk. Consider safer methods to store sensitive data.
- **Public networks** may expose your device to security threats.

2. Checking Wi-Fi Connection Status Using `WiFi.status()`

What is `WiFi.status()`?

`WiFi.status()` checks whether the ESP32 is connected to a Wi-Fi network. It returns status codes such as `WL_CONNECTED` for a successful connection or `WL_DISCONNECTED` if not connected.

Use Purpose

The function helps to:

- **Verify the connection status** before performing tasks that require network access.
- **Troubleshoot connectivity issues** by providing status information.

Arduino Syntax Use
`WiFi.status();`

Arduino Syntax Explanation

1. `WiFi`: Refers to the built-in Wi-Fi library for ESP32. This library handles the connection, configuration, and management of the Wi-Fi interface.
2. `status()`: A function within the Wi-Fi library that returns the current connection status. It provides different status codes indicating the connection state:
    - `WL_CONNECTED`: The ESP32 is successfully connected to a Wi-Fi network.
    - `WL_DISCONNECTED`: The ESP32 is not connected to any Wi-Fi network.
    - `WL_NO_SSID_AVAIL`: The configured SSID is not available within range.
    - `WL_CONNECT_FAILED`: The connection to the network failed, possibly due to incorrect credentials.
    - `WL_IDLE_STATUS`: The Wi-Fi is in an idle state and not currently active.
3. **Return Value**: The function returns an integer corresponding to the connection status. These status codes are predefined constants in the Wi-Fi library.

Arduino Simple Code Example

```cpp
#include <WiFi.h>

const char* ssid = "Your_SSID";
const char* password = "Your_PASSWORD";

void setup() {
  Serial.begin(115200);
  WiFi.begin(ssid, password);

  // Check connection status
  if (WiFi.status() == WL_CONNECTED) {
    Serial.println("Wi-Fi is connected.");
  } else {
    Serial.println("Wi-Fi is not connected.");
  }
}

void loop() {
  // Main code here
}
```

Notes

- WiFi.status() can be used to detect if a connection is lost and attempt reconnection.
- Helpful for continuously monitoring the network status in a loop.

Warnings

- **Unstable networks** can cause frequent status changes.
- Implement error handling to manage connection loss gracefully.

3. Disconnecting from Wi-Fi Using WiFi.disconnect()

What is WiFi.disconnect()?

WiFi.disconnect() disconnects the ESP32 from the current Wi-Fi network in Station Mode.

Use Purpose

The function is useful for:

- **Switching between networks without restarting** the ESP32.
- **Reducing power consumption** by disconnecting when Wi-Fi is not needed.

Arduino Syntax Use
WiFi.disconnect();

Arduino Syntax Explanation

1. **WiFi**: Refers to the Wi-Fi library used for managing wireless connectivity.
2. **disconnect()**: This function terminates the current Wi-Fi connection and puts the Wi-Fi interface in a disconnected state. It can be used to:
    - **End ongoing network activities** (e.g., data transfers).
    - **Release the IP address** assigned by the DHCP server.
    - **Free up resources** associated with the connection.
3. **Return Value**: The function does not return a value. To confirm disconnection, you can check the connection status using WiFi.status().

Arduino Simple Code Example

```
#include <WiFi.h>

void setup() {
  Serial.begin(115200);
```

```
WiFi.disconnect();
Serial.println("Disconnected from Wi-Fi.");
}

void loop() {
  // Main code here
}
```

Notes

- After disconnecting, use WiFi.begin() to reconnect.
- Helps save battery power for mobile applications.

Warnings

- **Disconnecting will interrupt any ongoing network communication.**
- Ensure that the device is not performing critical tasks over the network before disconnecting.

---

4. Getting Local IP Address Using WiFi.localIP()

What is WiFi.localIP()?

WiFi.localIP() retrieves the local IP address assigned to the ESP32 when it is connected to a Wi-Fi network. This IP address is typically assigned by the network's DHCP server.

Use Purpose

The function is used to:

- **Identify the IP address of the ESP32** on the local network.
- **Enable communication with the ESP32** over the network (e.g., for a web server or IoT application).
- **Debug network connections** by checking the assigned IP address.

Arduino Syntax Use

```
WiFi.localIP();
```

Arduino Syntax Explanation

1. **WiFi**: Refers to the built-in Wi-Fi library for the ESP32. It provides functions for managing Wi-Fi connections, including obtaining network information.
2. **localIP()**: A function that returns the local IP address assigned to the ESP32. The returned IP address is of type IPAddress and represents the device's address within the local network.
    - **Purpose**: Allows you to know the device's network address, which is useful for setting up web servers or network-based applications.
3. **Return Value**: The function returns an IPAddress object containing the current local IP address. If the device is not connected to a Wi-Fi network, it returns 0.0.0.0.

Arduino Simple Code Example

```
#include <WiFi.h>

const char* ssid = "Your_SSID";
const char* password = "Your_PASSWORD";

void setup() {
  Serial.begin(115200);
  WiFi.begin(ssid, password);

  while (WiFi.status() != WL_CONNECTED) {
    delay(500);
  }

  // Print the local IP address
  Serial.print("Local IP: ");
  Serial.println(WiFi.localIP());
}

void loop() {
  // Main code here
}
```

Notes

- The IP address is usually assigned by the router's DHCP server when the ESP32 connects to the network.
- Knowing the local IP is essential for developing applications like web servers or remote control setups.

Warnings

- If the ESP32 is not connected to a network, WiFi.localIP() will return 0.0.0.0.
- Avoid exposing the IP address in public environments without securing the network.

---

5. Reconnecting to Wi-Fi Using WiFi.reconnect()

What is WiFi.reconnect()?

WiFi.reconnect() attempts to reconnect the ESP32 to the last known Wi-Fi network. This can be useful if the device was previously connected but lost the connection.

Use Purpose

The function is used to:

- **Re-establish a lost connection** without resetting the device.
- **Maintain continuous network connectivity** for long-running tasks or critical applications.
- **Handle temporary disconnections automatically.**

Arduino Syntax Use
WiFi.reconnect();

Arduino Syntax Explanation

1. **WiFi**: Represents the Wi-Fi library for ESP32, which provides functions for managing network connections.
2. **reconnect()**: A function that initiates a reconnection attempt to the previously connected Wi-Fi network.

- **What it does**: If the ESP32 was connected to a network but lost the connection, this function will try to re-establish the connection using the same SSID and password.
- **Useful for**: Scenarios where the connection drops momentarily due to signal loss or network issues.
3. **Return Value**: The function does not return a value. To check if the reconnection was successful, use WiFi.status() after calling WiFi.reconnect().

Arduino Simple Code Example

```
#include <WiFi.h>

const char* ssid = "Your_SSID";
const char* password = "Your_PASSWORD";

void setup() {
  Serial.begin(115200);
  WiFi.begin(ssid, password);

  // Attempt to reconnect if the connection is lost
  if (WiFi.status() != WL_CONNECTED) {
    WiFi.reconnect();
    Serial.println("Reconnecting to Wi-Fi...");
  } else {
    Serial.println("Already connected.");
  }
}

void loop() {
  // Main code here
}
```

Notes

- Reconnecting is useful for recovering from temporary network failures.
- It is helpful in maintaining a stable connection for critical applications.

Warnings

- Reconnection attempts may fail if the network is not available or the credentials have changed.
- Use appropriate error handling to manage repeated reconnection attempts.

---

6. Checking if Connected Using WiFi.isConnected()

What is WiFi.isConnected()?

WiFi.isConnected() checks whether the ESP32 is currently connected to a Wi-Fi network. It returns true if the connection is active and false if it is not.

Use Purpose

The function is used to:

- **Verify network connectivity** before performing tasks that require an active connection.
- **Prevent errors** related to network unavailability.
- **Monitor connection stability** during long-running tasks.

Arduino Syntax Use
WiFi.isConnected();

Arduino Syntax Explanation

1. **WiFi**: Refers to the built-in Wi-Fi library used for handling network-related tasks on the ESP32.
2. **isConnected()**: A function that returns a Boolean value indicating the connection status.
   - **Returns true**: If the ESP32 is currently connected to a Wi-Fi network.
   - **Returns false**: If the device is not connected to any network.
3. **Return Value**: The function returns a Boolean (true or false) based on the current connection status.

Arduino Simple Code Example
#include <WiFi.h>

```cpp
const char* ssid = "Your_SSID";
const char* password = "Your_PASSWORD";

void setup() {
  Serial.begin(115200);
  WiFi.begin(ssid, password);

  while (WiFi.status() != WL_CONNECTED) {
    delay(500);
  }

  // Check if connected
  if (WiFi.isConnected()) {
    Serial.println("Wi-Fi is connected.");
  } else {
    Serial.println("Wi-Fi is not connected.");
  }
}

void loop() {
  // Main code here
}
```

Notes

- Use this function to confirm connectivity before attempting network-dependent tasks.
- Can be used in conjunction with `WiFi.reconnect()` to handle connection loss.

Warnings

- A network connection may still drop unexpectedly even if `WiFi.isConnected()` initially returns `true`.
- Make sure to have a retry mechanism for network tasks in case of disconnection.

7. Scanning for Available Networks Using WiFi.scanNetworks()

What is WiFi.scanNetworks()?

WiFi.scanNetworks() searches for nearby Wi-Fi networks and returns the number of available networks found. This function is useful for finding and connecting to available networks.

Use Purpose

The function is used to:

- **List all Wi-Fi networks** within range of the ESP32.
- **Display network details**, such as SSID and signal strength.
- **Assist in selecting the best network** based on signal quality or other criteria.

Arduino Syntax Use

WiFi.scanNetworks();

Arduino Syntax Explanation

1. **WiFi**: Refers to the built-in Wi-Fi library for the ESP32, which provides networking functionalities.
2. **scanNetworks()**: A function that performs a scan to detect nearby Wi-Fi networks.
   - **What it does**: Returns the number of networks found and stores information about each network, including SSID, signal strength (RSSI), encryption type, and whether the network is hidden.
   - **Usage**: Typically used to present a list of available networks for the user to choose from.
3. **Return Value**: The function returns an integer indicating the number of networks found during the scan.

Arduino Simple Code Example

```
#include <WiFi.h>

void setup() {
  Serial.begin(115200);
```

```
// Perform a network scan
int numberOfNetworks = WiFi.scanNetworks();
Serial.println("Scan complete.");

// Display the networks found
for (int i = 0; i < numberOfNetworks; i++) {
  Serial.print("Network Name (SSID): ");
  Serial.println(WiFi.SSID(i));
  Serial.print("Signal Strength (RSSI): ");
  Serial.println(WiFi.RSSI(i));
  Serial.println("------------------------");
}
}

void loop() {
  // Main code here
}
```

Notes

- Scanning for networks can take a few seconds to complete.
- Useful for debugging connectivity issues by checking the network environment.

Warnings

- Repeated scans can consume significant power and network resources.
- Some networks may be hidden and will not appear in the scan results.

Complete Real-Life Simple Project Code for This Chapter

Project Name: ESP32 Wi-Fi Connection Monitor

Project Goal

- **Connect to a Wi-Fi network using Station Mode on ESP32.**
- **Check the connection status and display it on the Serial Monitor.**
- **Retrieve and display the local IP address upon a successful connection.**

Project Code

```cpp
#include <WiFi.h>

// Wi-Fi credentials
const char* ssid = "Your_SSID";           // Replace with
your network's SSID
const char* password = "Your_PASSWORD";   // Replace with
your network's password

void setup() {
  Serial.begin(115200);

  // Step 1: Connect to Wi-Fi
  WiFi.begin(ssid, password);
  Serial.print("Connecting to Wi-Fi");
  while (WiFi.status() != WL_CONNECTED) {
    delay(500);
    Serial.print(".");
  }
  Serial.println("\nConnected to Wi-Fi!");

  // Step 2: Display connection status and local IP address
  if (WiFi.status() == WL_CONNECTED) {
    Serial.println("Wi-Fi connection successful.");
    Serial.print("Local IP: ");
    Serial.println(WiFi.localIP());
  } else {
    Serial.println("Wi-Fi connection failed.");
  }

  // Step 3: Disconnect from Wi-Fi
  WiFi.disconnect();
  Serial.println("Disconnected from Wi-Fi.");
```

```
}

void loop() {
  // No code needed for the loop in this example
}
```

Save and Run

1. **Open the Arduino IDE** and create a new sketch.
2. **Copy the project code** above into the new sketch.
3. **Connect your ESP32** to your computer via USB.
4. **Configure the Arduino IDE**:
   o   Go to **Tools > Board** and select **ESP32 Dev Module**.
   o   Go to **Tools > Port** and choose the appropriate COM port.
5. **Upload the code** by clicking on the **Upload button**.

Check Output

1. **Open the Serial Monitor** in the Arduino IDE (Tools > Serial Monitor).
2. **Set the baud rate** to **115200**.
3. You should see messages indicating:
   o   **Connecting to Wi-Fi** with progress dots.
   o   **Connected to Wi-Fi** and the **local IP address**.
   o   **Disconnected from Wi-Fi** after completing the steps.

```
Connecting to Wi-Fi..
Connected to Wi-Fi!
Wi-Fi connection successful.
Local IP: 192.168.0.103
Disconnected from Wi-Fi.
```

This complete guide to **Station Mode on ESP32** provides a comprehensive understanding of how to connect to Wi-Fi networks, manage the connection, and monitor network status.

8.2. Access Point Mode (AP) on ESP32

In this chapter, you'll learn how to set up **Access Point Mode (AP) on ESP32** to create a Wi-Fi network. In Access Point Mode, the ESP32 acts as a Wi-Fi hotspot, allowing other devices to connect directly to it without requiring an external router. This guide covers the basic functions for configuring an access point, setting the network SSID and password, and handling connected clients. You'll also find a simple project to demonstrate how to set up Access Point Mode on ESP32.

What is Access Point Mode (AP) on ESP32?

Access Point Mode, or AP Mode, allows the ESP32 to create its own Wi-Fi network, which other devices can join. When the ESP32 is configured as an access point, it can:

- **Create a local Wi-Fi network** that devices like smartphones, laptops, and other IoT devices can connect to.
- **Share data and communicate** directly with connected devices without needing an internet connection.
- **Act as a local server** for web-based interfaces or remote control applications.

Syntax Table for Access Point Functions on ESP32

Seri al No.	Topic	Syntax	Simple Example
1	**Set Up Access Point**	WiFi.softAP(ssid, password)	WiFi.softAP("MyESP32A P", "MyPassword123");
2	**Get AP IP Addres s**	WiFi.softAPIP()	IPAddress apIP = WiFi.softAPIP();
3	**Check Connec ted Clients**	WiFi.softAPgetStati onNum()	int clients = WiFi.softAPgetStation Num();
4	**Stop Access Point**	WiFi.softAPdisconne ct()	WiFi.softAPdisconnect (true);

This table provides a quick reference to key functions for setting up **Access Point Mode on ESP32**, making it easier to create and manage a Wi-Fi network.

---

1. Setting Up Access Point Using WiFi.softAP(ssid, password)

What is WiFi.softAP(ssid, password)?

WiFi.softAP(ssid, password) is the function used to configure the ESP32 as an access point. It allows the ESP32 to create its own Wi-Fi network with the given SSID (network name) and password.

Use Purpose

This function is used to:

- **Create a Wi-Fi network** that other devices can connect to.
- **Enable local communication** between the ESP32 and connected devices.
- **Set up a local server** for web-based control or monitoring.

Arduino Syntax Use

```
WiFi.softAP(ssid, password);
```

Arduino Syntax Explanation

1. **WiFi**: This refers to the built-in Wi-Fi library for the ESP32. It provides various functions to set up and manage both Station and Access Point Modes.
2. **softAP()**: This function sets up the ESP32 as an access point.
    - **What it does**: It configures the ESP32 to create a Wi-Fi network using the specified SSID and password, allowing other devices to connect directly to the ESP32.
    - **Usage**: Can be used for creating local IoT networks or for situations where the ESP32 needs to act as a local server.
3. **ssid**: This parameter specifies the SSID (network name) for the access point.
    - **Data Type**: const char* (a string in C++)
    - **Purpose**: Sets the name of the Wi-Fi network that other devices will see and connect to.
4. **password**: This parameter sets the password for the access point.
    - **Data Type**: const char* (a string in C++)
    - **Purpose**: Adds security to the network, ensuring only authorized users can connect. If the password is set to an empty string (""), the network will be open (not recommended for security reasons).
5. **Return Value**: The function returns a Boolean indicating whether the access point was successfully set up.

Arduino Simple Code Example

```
#include <WiFi.h>

// Access Point credentials
const char* ssid = "MyESP32AP";            // Network name
const char* password = "MyPassword123";    // Network password

void setup() {
  Serial.begin(115200);

  // Set up the access point
  if (WiFi.softAP(ssid, password)) {
    Serial.println("Access Point Created");
    Serial.print("AP IP address: ");
    Serial.println(WiFi.softAPIP());
  } else {
    Serial.println("Failed to create Access Point");
  }
}

void loop() {
  // Main code here
}
```

Notes

- The SSID and password should be unique and secure.
- The password must be at least 8 characters long if used.

Warnings

- **Open networks** (no password) may pose security risks, as anyone can connect.
- **Using simple passwords** may allow unauthorized access.

2. Getting the Access Point IP Address Using `WiFi.softAPIP()`

What is `WiFi.softAPIP()`?

`WiFi.softAPIP()` retrieves the IP address assigned to the ESP32 access point. This IP is used by other devices to connect to the ESP32 over the network.

Use Purpose

The function is used to:

- **Identify the IP address of the ESP32** on the network.
- **Enable other devices** to communicate with the ESP32.
- **Set up local servers** where the IP address is needed.

Arduino Syntax Use
`WiFi.softAPIP();`

Arduino Syntax Explanation

1. **WiFi**: Refers to the built-in Wi-Fi library used for managing Wi-Fi functionalities on the ESP32.
2. **softAPIP()**: A function that returns the IP address assigned to the ESP32 in Access Point Mode.
   - **What it does**: Provides the IP address used by clients to communicate with the ESP32 over the Wi-Fi network.
   - **Usage**: Useful when setting up a web server on the ESP32 or when other devices need to connect to the ESP32 using its IP address.
3. **Return Value**: The function returns an `IPAddress` object containing the IP address.

Arduino Simple Code Example
```
#include <WiFi.h>

const char* ssid = "MyESP32AP";
const char* password = "MyPassword123";

void setup() {
```

```
  Serial.begin(115200);

  WiFi.softAP(ssid, password);

  // Display the IP address of the access point
  Serial.print("Access Point IP Address: ");
  Serial.println(WiFi.softAPIP());
}

void loop() {
  // Main code here
}
```

Notes

- By default, the IP address of the ESP32 access point is 192.168.4.1.
- The IP address can be configured manually using WiFi.softAPConfig().

Warnings

- Changing the default IP address might cause connectivity issues if not done correctly.
- Avoid using the same IP address range as your main network to prevent conflicts.

---

3. Checking the Number of Connected Clients Using WiFi.softAPgetStationNum()

What is WiFi.softAPgetStationNum()?

WiFi.softAPgetStationNum() returns the number of devices currently connected to the ESP32's access point.

Use Purpose

This function is used to:

- **Monitor how many clients** are connected to the ESP32.
- **Control the number of connections** to manage network load.
- **Trigger actions** when a certain number of devices are connected.

Arduino Syntax Use

```
WiFi.softAPgetStationNum();
```

Arduino Syntax Explanation

1. **WiFi**: Represents the Wi-Fi library for the ESP32, which handles network functionalities.
2. **softAPgetStationNum()**: A function that returns the number of devices connected to the ESP32's access point.
   - **What it does**: Allows the program to know how many clients are currently connected.
   - **Usage**: Useful for monitoring network activity and controlling access to resources.
3. **Return Value**: The function returns an integer representing the number of connected devices.

Arduino Simple Code Example

```
#include <WiFi.h>

const char* ssid = "MyESP32AP";
const char* password = "MyPassword123";

void setup() {
  Serial.begin(115200);

  WiFi.softAP(ssid, password);

  // Display the number of connected clients
  Serial.print("Number of connected clients: ");
  Serial.println(WiFi.softAPgetStationNum());
}

void loop() {
  // Main code here
```

}

Notes

- The function can be used in a loop to continuously monitor the number of connected devices.
- It is helpful for limiting the number of clients to avoid network overload.

Warnings

- Allowing too many clients to connect may affect the ESP32's performance.
- Be aware of your network's capacity when handling multiple connections.

---

4. Stopping the Access Point Using WiFi.softAPdisconnect()

What is WiFi.softAPdisconnect()?

WiFi.softAPdisconnect() is used to stop the ESP32's access point, disconnecting all connected clients.

Use Purpose

This function is used to:

- **Stop the access point** when it is no longer needed.
- **Disconnect all connected devices** from the ESP32.
- **Conserve power** by turning off the Wi-Fi network.

Arduino Syntax Use
WiFi.softAPdisconnect(wifioff);

Arduino Syntax Explanation

1. **WiFi**: The library used to manage Wi-Fi functionalities on the ESP32.
2. **softAPdisconnect()**: This function stops the access point.

- What it does: Disables the access point and disconnects all currently connected clients.
- Usage: Use this when the access point is no longer required or to reset the network.
3. **wifioff (optional)**: A Boolean parameter that specifies whether to turn off the Wi-Fi interface entirely.
   - **true**: Turns off the Wi-Fi interface.
   - **false**: Keeps the Wi-Fi interface on, but stops the access point.
4. **Return Value**: The function does not return a value.

Arduino Simple Code Example

```
#include <WiFi.h>
void setup() {
  Serial.begin(115200);
    WiFi.softAP("MyESP32AP", "MyPassword123");
    delay(5000); // Let the access point run for 5 seconds
    // Stop the access point
  WiFi.softAPdisconnect(true);
  Serial.println("Access Point Stopped");
}
void loop() {
  // Main code here
}
```

Notes

- Stopping the access point will disconnect all connected clients.
- It can be used as part of a power-saving strategy.

Warnings

- Ensure that all important tasks are completed before disconnecting.
- Stopping the access point may disrupt network-related tasks.

Complete Real-Life Project Code for This Chapter

Project Name: ESP32 Basic Access Point

Project Goal

- **Create a simple Wi-Fi network** with ESP32 as the access point.
- **Display the access point's IP address.**
- **Monitor the number of connected clients** and print it to the Serial Monitor.
- **Stop the access point after a specified duration.**

Project Code

```cpp
#include <WiFi.h>

// Access Point credentials
const char* ssid = "MyESP32AP";
const char* password = "MyPassword123";

void setup() {
  Serial.begin(115200);

  // Set up the access point
  if (WiFi.softAP(ssid, password)) {
    Serial.println("Access Point Created");
    Serial.print("AP IP Address: ");
    Serial.println(WiFi.softAPIP());
  } else {
    Serial.println("Failed to create Access Point");
  }

  // Monitor the number of connected clients
  Serial.print("Number of connected clients: ");
  Serial.println(WiFi.softAPgetStationNum());

  // Let the access point run for 10 seconds
  delay(10000);

  // Stop the access point
```

```
  //WiFi.softAPdisconnect(true);
  // Serial.println("Access Point Stopped");
}

void loop() {
  // No code needed for the loop in this example
}
```

Save and Run

1. **Open the Arduino IDE** and create a new sketch.
2. **Copy the project code** above into the new sketch.
3. **Connect your ESP32** to your computer via USB.
4. **Configure the Arduino IDE**:
   - Go to **Tools > Board** and select **ESP32 Dev Module**.
   - Go to **Tools > Port** and choose the appropriate COM port.
5. **Upload the code** by clicking on the **Upload button**.

Check Output

1. **Open the Serial Monitor** in the Arduino IDE (Tools > Serial Monitor).
2. **Set the baud rate** to **115200**.
3. The Serial Monitor should display:
   - **Access Point creation status**.
   - **IP address of the Access Point**.
   - **Number of connected clients**.
   - **Access Point status** after stopping.

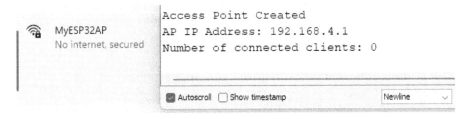

This project demonstrates the basics of using **Access Point Mode on ESP32**, including creating a Wi-Fi network, monitoring clients, and stopping the network when needed.

8.3 Station + Access Point Mode (STA+AP) on ESP32

In this chapter, you'll learn how to configure the ESP32 to operate in **Station + Access Point Mode (STA+AP)**. This dual-mode configuration allows the ESP32 to connect to an existing Wi-Fi network as a client (Station Mode) while simultaneously acting as an access point to create its own Wi-Fi network. This setup enables the ESP32 to communicate with other devices on a local network while allowing direct connections from nearby devices. We will cover essential functions for configuring STA+AP Mode, followed by a simple project example to illustrate how to implement it.

What is Station + Access Point Mode (STA+AP) on ESP32?

Station + Access Point Mode (STA+AP) combines the functionalities of Station Mode and Access Point Mode:

- **Station Mode (STA)**: The ESP32 connects to an existing Wi-Fi network, such as a home or office router.
- **Access Point Mode (AP)**: The ESP32 creates its own Wi-Fi network, allowing other devices to connect directly to it.

When configured in STA+AP Mode, the ESP32 can simultaneously:

- **Connect to an existing Wi-Fi network** to access the internet or communicate with other devices on the network.
- **Create its own Wi-Fi network** for local devices to connect and communicate directly.

This dual-mode configuration is useful for IoT applications where the ESP32 needs to interact with both local devices and a remote server.

Syntax Table for STA+AP Mode Functions

Serial No.	Topic	Syntax	Simple Example
1	Set Up STA+AP Mode	WiFi.begin(ssid, password) and WiFi.softAP(ap_ssid, ap_password)	WiFi.begin("MyNetwork", "NetworkPassword"); WiFi.softAP("ESP32AP", "ESP32Password");
2	Get STA IP Address	WiFi.localIP()	IPAddress staIP = WiFi.localIP();
3	Get AP IP Address	WiFi.softAPIP()	IPAddress apIP = WiFi.softAPIP();
4	Monitor Connected Clients	WiFi.softAPgetStationNum()	int clients = WiFi.softAPgetStationNum();
5	Stop the Access Point	WiFi.softAPdisconnect()	WiFi.softAPdisconnect(true);

This table summarizes the main functions used to configure and manage **Station + Access Point Mode (STA+AP) on ESP32**.

1. Setting Up STA+AP Mode Using WiFi.begin() and WiFi.softAP()

What is STA+AP Mode Setup?

To configure the ESP32 in STA+AP Mode, you need to set up the device to connect to an existing Wi-Fi network using `WiFi.begin(ssid, password)` for Station Mode, and simultaneously create a new access point using `WiFi.softAP(ap_ssid, ap_password)` for Access Point Mode.

Use Purpose

This configuration allows the ESP32 to:

- **Connect to a local Wi-Fi network** for internet access or interaction with other devices.
- **Create a separate local Wi-Fi network** for nearby devices to connect directly to the ESP32.
- **Enable remote communication** with devices connected to the local network and nearby clients.

Arduino Syntax Use

```
WiFi.begin(sta_ssid, sta_password);
WiFi.softAP(ap_ssid, ap_password);
```

Arduino Syntax Explanation

1. **WiFi**: Refers to the built-in Wi-Fi library for the ESP32. It provides functions to configure both Station Mode and Access Point Mode.
2. **begin() for STA**: This function connects the ESP32 to an existing Wi-Fi network in Station Mode.
   - **Parameters**:
     - sta_ssid: The SSID of the existing Wi-Fi network.
     - sta_password: The password of the existing Wi-Fi network.
   - **Purpose**: Connects the ESP32 to an external router for internet access or communication with other devices.
3. **softAP() for AP**: This function creates a new Wi-Fi network with the ESP32 as the access point.
   - **Parameters**:
     - ap_ssid: The SSID of the access point.

- ap_password: The password of the access point.
  - **Purpose**: Allows nearby devices to connect directly to the ESP32's Wi-Fi network.
4. **Return Value**: These functions do not return any values. To confirm successful connections, check the status using WiFi.status() and verify the access point with WiFi.softAPIP().

Arduino Simple Code Example

```
#include <WiFi.h>

// Station Mode (STA) credentials
const char* sta_ssid = "MyNetwork";
const char* sta_password = "NetworkPassword";

// Access Point (AP) credentials
const char* ap_ssid = "ESP32AP";
const char* ap_password = "ESP32Password";

void setup() {
  Serial.begin(115200);

  // Set up STA+AP Mode
  WiFi.begin(sta_ssid, sta_password);   // Connect to
existing network
  WiFi.softAP(ap_ssid, ap_password);    // Create access
point

  Serial.println("ESP32 in STA+AP Mode");

  // Display STA IP Address
  Serial.print("STA IP Address: ");
  Serial.println(WiFi.localIP());

  // Display AP IP Address
  Serial.print("AP IP Address: ");
  Serial.println(WiFi.softAPIP());
}
```

```
void loop() {
  // Main code here
}
```

Notes

- The ESP32 can act as both a client and access point simultaneously in STA+AP Mode.
- The SSID and password for both Station Mode and Access Point Mode should be different to avoid conflicts.

Warnings

- **Open networks (without a password)** may pose security risks, especially for the access point.
- **Weak passwords** may allow unauthorized connections.

---

2. Getting the Station Mode IP Address Using WiFi.localIP()

What is WiFi.localIP()?

WiFi.localIP() retrieves the IP address assigned to the ESP32 when it is connected to an existing Wi-Fi network in Station Mode.

Use Purpose

This function is used to:

- **Identify the IP address** of the ESP32 on the local network.
- **Enable communication** between the ESP32 and other devices on the same network.
- **Debug network connectivity issues** by checking the assigned IP.

Arduino Syntax Use

```
WiFi.localIP();
```

Arduino Syntax Explanation

1. **WiFi**: Represents the built-in library for Wi-Fi management on the ESP32.
2. **localIP()**: This function returns the IP address assigned to the ESP32 in Station Mode.
   - **Return Value**: Returns an IPAddress object containing the IP address of the ESP32 within the local network.

Arduino Simple Code Example

```
#include <WiFi.h>

void setup() {
  Serial.begin(115200);
  WiFi.begin("MyNetwork", "NetworkPassword");

  while (WiFi.status() != WL_CONNECTED) {
    delay(500);
    Serial.print(".");
  }

  // Display the IP address assigned in STA Mode
  Serial.print("Connected to STA network. IP Address: ");
  Serial.println(WiFi.localIP());
}

void loop() {
  // Main code here
}
```

Notes

- The IP address is typically assigned by the network's DHCP server.
- Useful for connecting the ESP32 to cloud servers or remote services.

Warnings

- If the ESP32 is not connected to the network, WiFi.localIP() will return 0.0.0.0.
- Ensure the network settings (SSID, password) are correct to avoid connection issues.

---

3. Getting the Access Point IP Address Using WiFi.softAPIP()

What is WiFi.softAPIP()?

WiFi.softAPIP() retrieves the IP address assigned to the ESP32 in Access Point Mode. This IP address is used by other devices to connect to the ESP32 over the access point.

Use Purpose

The function is used to:

- **Identify the IP address of the ESP32's access point**.
- **Enable direct connections** from nearby devices.
- **Set up a local server** hosted on the ESP32.

Arduino Syntax Use
WiFi.softAPIP();

Arduino Syntax Explanation

1. **WiFi**: Refers to the built-in Wi-Fi library for the ESP32, which manages network configurations.
2. **softAPIP()**: A function that returns the IP address used by the ESP32 when it operates in Access Point Mode.

- o **Return Value**: Returns an IPAddress object containing the IP address of the access point.

Arduino Simple Code Example

```
#include <WiFi.h>

void setup() {
  Serial.begin(115200);
  WiFi.softAP("ESP32AP", "ESP32Password");

  // Display the IP address of the access point
  Serial.print("AP IP Address: ");
  Serial.println(WiFi.softAPIP());
}

void loop() {
  // Main code here
}
```

Notes

- By default, the IP address is set to 192. 168. 4. 1 for the ESP32 access point.
- You can configure a different IP address using WiFi.softAPConfig().

Warnings

- Changing the IP address configuration improperly may cause connectivity issues.
- Avoid setting the same IP address for the STA and AP networks.

---

4. Monitoring the Number of Connected Clients Using WiFi.softAPgetStationNum()

What is WiFi.softAPgetStationNum()?

`WiFi.softAPgetStationNum()` returns the number of devices currently connected to the ESP32's access point.

Use Purpose

The function is used to:

- **Monitor the number of clients** connected to the ESP32.
- **Control access** by limiting the number of connections.
- **Trigger actions** based on the number of connected clients.

Arduino Syntax Use
`WiFi.softAPgetStationNum();`

Arduino Syntax Explanation

1. **WiFi**: Represents the built-in Wi-Fi library for the ESP32.
2. **softAPgetStationNum()**: A function that returns the number of devices connected to the access point.
   - **Return Value**: Returns an integer representing the number of connected clients.

Arduino Simple Code Example

```
#include <WiFi.h>

void setup() {
  Serial.begin(115200);
  WiFi.softAP("ESP32AP", "ESP32Password");

  // Print the number of connected clients
  Serial.print("Number of connected clients: ");
  Serial.println(WiFi.softAPgetStationNum());
}

void loop() {
  // Main code here
}
```

Notes

- Can be used to dynamically manage network traffic.
- Useful for limiting the number of devices that can connect.

Warnings

- Allowing too many connections may slow down network performance.
- Be mindful of the network capacity when monitoring multiple connections.

---

5. Stopping the Access Point Using WiFi.softAPdisconnect()

What is WiFi.softAPdisconnect()?

WiFi.softAPdisconnect() stops the access point and disconnects all connected devices.

Use Purpose

This function is used to:

- **Stop the access point** when it is no longer needed.
- **Disconnect all devices** from the ESP32.
- **Conserve power** by shutting down the Wi-Fi interface.

Arduino Syntax Use

WiFi.softAPdisconnect(wifioff);

Arduino Syntax Explanation

1. **WiFi**: The built-in library for Wi-Fi management on the ESP32.
2. **softAPdisconnect()**: Stops the access point and disconnects all clients.
   - **wifioff (optional)**: A Boolean parameter that, if set to true, will also turn off the Wi-Fi interface.
   - **Return Value**: Does not return a value.

Arduino Simple Code Example

```
#include <WiFi.h>

void setup() {
  Serial.begin(115200);
  WiFi.softAP("ESP32AP", "ESP32Password");

  delay(10000); // Run the access point for 10 seconds

  // Stop the access point
  WiFi.softAPdisconnect(true);
  Serial.println("Access Point Stopped");
}

void loop() {
  // Main code here
}
```

Notes

- Stopping the access point will disconnect all connected clients.
- The ESP32 can still be connected to a Wi-Fi network in Station Mode.

Warnings

- Ensure critical tasks are completed before stopping the access point.
- Disabling the Wi-Fi interface may affect ongoing network activities.

Complete Real-Life Project Code for STA+AP Mode

Project Name: Dual-Mode ESP32 Network

Project Goal

- **Connect the ESP32 to an existing Wi-Fi network** using Station Mode.
- **Create an access point for local devices** to connect directly.
- **Display the IP addresses for both Station Mode and Access Point Mode**.
- **Monitor the number of connected clients** and stop the access point after 20 seconds.

Project Code

```
#include <WiFi.h>

// Station Mode (STA) credentials
const char* sta_ssid = "MyNetwork";
const char* sta_password = "NetworkPassword";

// Access Point (AP) credentials
const char* ap_ssid = "ESP32AP";
const char* ap_password = "ESP32Password";

void setup() {
  Serial.begin(115200);

  // Set up STA+AP Mode
  WiFi.begin(sta_ssid, sta_password);  // Connect to existing network
  WiFi.softAP(ap_ssid, ap_password);   // Create access point

  Serial.println("ESP32 in STA+AP Mode");

  // Display STA IP Address
  Serial.print("STA IP Address: ");
  Serial.println(WiFi.localIP());
```

```
// Display AP IP Address
Serial.print("AP IP Address: ");
Serial.println(WiFi.softAPIP());

// Monitor the number of connected clients
Serial.print("Number of connected clients: ");
Serial.println(WiFi.softAPgetStationNum());

// Run the access point for 20 seconds
delay(20000);

// Stop the access point
WiFi.softAPdisconnect(true);
Serial.println("Access Point Stopped");
}

void loop() {
    // No code needed for the loop in this example
}
```

Save and Run

1. **Open the Arduino IDE** and create a new sketch.
2. **Copy the project code** above into the new sketch.
3. **Connect your ESP32** to your computer via USB.
4. **Configure the Arduino IDE**:
   - Go to **Tools > Board** and select **ESP32 Dev Module**.
   - Go to **Tools > Port** and choose the appropriate COM port.
5. **Upload the code** by clicking on the **Upload button**.

Check Output

1. **Open the Serial Monitor** in the Arduino IDE (Tools > Serial Monitor).
2. **Set the baud rate** to **115200**.
3. The Serial Monitor should display:

- ESP32 dual-mode configuration status.
- IP addresses for both Station Mode and Access Point Mode.
- Number of connected clients.
- Status of the access point after stopping.

```
ESP32 in STA+AP Mode
STA IP Address: 0.0.0.0
AP IP Address: 192.168.4.1
Number of connected clients: 0
```

This project demonstrates how to configure the ESP32 to operate in **Station + Access Point Mode (STA+AP)**, allowing it to connect to a Wi-Fi network while creating a separate local network for nearby devices.

8.4. Wi-Fi Scan on ESP32

In this guide, you'll learn how to perform a **Wi-Fi Scan on ESP32**, a feature that allows the microcontroller to detect nearby Wi-Fi networks. This tutorial is designed for absolute beginners who want to understand the basics of scanning for available networks using the ESP32. We'll cover essential functions to scan, list, and retrieve details about detected networks, along with a practical project example to demonstrate how to implement a Wi-Fi scan on the ESP32.

What is a Wi-Fi Scan on ESP32?

A **Wi-Fi Scan on ESP32** involves searching for available wireless networks within range of the device. The ESP32 can detect network names (SSIDs), signal strengths (RSSI), encryption types, and other details. This functionality is useful for:

- **Listing available networks** to choose the best one for connecting.
- **Monitoring network signal strength** for troubleshooting.
- **Identifying open networks** or secure networks nearby.

Syntax Table for Wi-Fi Scan Functions

Serial No.	Topic	Syntax	Simple Example
1	**Start a Wi-Fi Scan**	`WiFi.scanNetworks()`	`int n = WiFi.scanNetworks();`
2	**Get Network SSID**	`WiFi.SSID(index)`	`String ssid = WiFi.SSID(i);`
3	**Get Network Signal Strength (RSSI)**	`WiFi.RSSI(index)`	`int rssi = WiFi.RSSI(i);`
4	**Get Encryption Type**	`WiFi.encryptionType(index)`	`int encryption = WiFi.encryptionType(i);`
5	**Check if a Network is Hidden**	`WiFi.isHidden(index)`	`bool hidden = WiFi.isHidden(i);`

This table provides an overview of the functions used to perform a **Wi-Fi Scan on ESP32**, enabling you to detect and retrieve information about nearby networks.

1. Starting a Wi-Fi Scan Using `WiFi.scanNetworks()`

What is `WiFi.scanNetworks()`?

`WiFi.scanNetworks()` initiates a scan for all available Wi-Fi networks within the range of the ESP32. It returns the number of networks found and makes the details of each network accessible.

Use Purpose

This function is used to:

- **Search for all nearby Wi-Fi networks** to get a list of available options.
- **Gather information about each network**, such as SSID, signal strength, and security type.
- **Troubleshoot network connectivity issues** by analyzing signal quality.

Arduino Syntax Use

```
int numNetworks = WiFi.scanNetworks();
```

Arduino Syntax Explanation

1. **WiFi**: Represents the built-in Wi-Fi library for the ESP32, which includes various functions for managing wireless connectivity.
2. **scanNetworks()**: A function that starts the scanning process to detect nearby Wi-Fi networks.
   - **What it does**: Returns an integer representing the number of networks found.
   - **Usage**: Can be called periodically to update the list of available networks.
3. **Return Value**: The function returns the number of networks detected during the scan. If no networks are found, it returns zero.

Arduino Simple Code Example

```
#include <WiFi.h>

void setup() {
  Serial.begin(115200);

  // Start the Wi-Fi scan
  int numberOfNetworks = WiFi.scanNetworks();
  Serial.print("Number of networks found: ");
  Serial.println(numberOfNetworks);
}

void loop() {
  // Main code here
}
```

Notes

- The scanning process may take a few seconds to complete.
- The ESP32 will list both visible and hidden networks (if detected).

Warnings

- Frequent scans can drain battery power in mobile applications.
- Scanning may interfere with other Wi-Fi tasks if done too often.

---

2. Retrieving the SSID of a Network Using WiFi.SSID(index)

What is WiFi.SSID(index)?

WiFi.SSID(index) returns the SSID (network name) of a Wi-Fi network found during the scan. The index refers to the position of the network in the list of detected networks.

Use Purpose

This function is used to:

- **Get the name of a Wi-Fi network** detected in the scan.
- **Display network names** to the user for choosing which network to connect to.
- **Log network information** for monitoring purposes.

Arduino Syntax Use

```
String ssid = WiFi.SSID(index);
```

Arduino Syntax Explanation

1. **WiFi**: Represents the Wi-Fi library that manages the network-related tasks on the ESP32.
2. **SSID()**: A function that retrieves the SSID (network name) of a specific Wi-Fi network from the list of scanned networks.
   - **Parameter index**: Indicates the position of the network in the list (0 to numberOfNetworks-1).
   - **Return Value**: Returns a String containing the SSID of the specified network.

Arduino Simple Code Example

```
#include <WiFi.h>

void setup() {
  Serial.begin(115200);

  int numberOfNetworks = WiFi.scanNetworks();
  Serial.println("Networks found:");

  for (int i = 0; i < numberOfNetworks; i++) {
    // Get and print the SSID of each network
    Serial.print("Network Name (SSID): ");
    Serial.println(WiFi.SSID(i));
  }
}

void loop() {
```

```
  // Main code here
}
```

Notes

- The SSID may be hidden or empty for some networks.
- Always check the number of networks before accessing an index.

Warnings

- The index must be within the valid range to avoid errors.
- Hidden networks may not reveal their SSID even if they are detected.

---

3. Getting the Signal Strength (RSSI) Using WiFi.RSSI(index)

What is WiFi.RSSI(index)?

WiFi.RSSI(index) retrieves the Received Signal Strength Indicator (RSSI) for a Wi-Fi network found during the scan. The RSSI value indicates the signal strength of the network.

Use Purpose

The function is used to:

- **Determine the strength of the Wi-Fi signal** for a specific network.
- **Help users choose the best network** based on signal quality.
- **Monitor changes in signal strength** for troubleshooting.

Arduino Syntax Use
```
int rssi = WiFi.RSSI(index);
```

Arduino Syntax Explanation

1. **WiFi**: Represents the Wi-Fi library used for handling Wi-Fi functions on the ESP32.

2. **RSSI ()**: A function that returns the signal strength of a specific Wi-Fi network in dBm.
   - **Parameter index**: Refers to the position of the network in the scanned list.
   - **Return Value**: Returns an integer value representing the RSSI in decibel-milliwatts (dBm). Higher values indicate stronger signals (e.g., -30 dBm is stronger than -70 dBm).

Arduino Simple Code Example

```
#include <WiFi.h>

void setup() {
  Serial.begin(115200);

  int numberOfNetworks = WiFi.scanNetworks();
  Serial.println("Networks found:");

  for (int i = 0; i < numberOfNetworks; i++) {
    // Print the SSID and signal strength of each network
    Serial.print("Network Name (SSID): ");
    Serial.print(WiFi.SSID(i));
    Serial.print(", Signal Strength (RSSI): ");
    Serial.println(WiFi.RSSI(i));
  }
}

void loop() {
  // Main code here
}
```

Notes

- RSSI values are usually negative. The closer to zero, the stronger the signal.
- Networks with high RSSI values provide better connectivity.

Warnings

- Signal strength can fluctuate due to environmental factors.
- Avoid connecting to networks with very weak signals (e.g., below -80 dBm).

---

4. Retrieving the Encryption Type Using WiFi.encryptionType(index)

What is WiFi.encryptionType(index)?

WiFi.encryptionType(index) returns the encryption type used by a Wi-Fi network found during the scan. It indicates whether the network is open, WEP-secured, WPA-secured, or WPA2-secured.

Use Purpose

The function is used to:

- **Identify the security type of each network.**
- **Determine whether a network is open or requires authentication.**
- **Choose the most secure network available.**

Arduino Syntax Use

```
int encryption = WiFi.encryptionType(index);
```

Arduino Syntax Explanation

1. **WiFi**: Represents the built-in Wi-Fi library for the ESP32.
2. **encryptionType ()**: A function that returns the encryption type used by the specified network.
   - **Parameter index**: Refers to the position of the network in the scanned list.
   - **Return Value**: Returns an integer representing the encryption type (e.g., WIFI_AUTH_OPEN, WIFI_AUTH_WEP, WIFI_AUTH_WPA_PSK, WIFI_AUTH_WPA2_PSK, etc.).

Arduino Simple Code Example

```
#include <WiFi.h>

void setup() {
  Serial.begin(115200);

  int numberOfNetworks = WiFi.scanNetworks();
  Serial.println("Networks found:");

  for (int i = 0; i < numberOfNetworks; i++) {
    // Print the SSID and encryption type of each network
    Serial.print("Network Name (SSID): ");
    Serial.print(WiFi.SSID(i));
    Serial.print(", Encryption Type: ");
    Serial.println(WiFi.encryptionType(i));
  }
}

void loop() {
  // Main code here
}
```

Notes

- Networks without encryption (WIFI_AUTH_OPEN) are not secure.
- Always prefer networks with WPA2 or higher encryption for better security.

Warnings

- Avoid connecting to open networks unless necessary.
- Use caution when accessing sensitive information on unsecured networks.

---

5. Checking if a Network is Hidden Using WiFi.isHidden(index)

What is `WiFi.isHidden(index)`?

`WiFi.isHidden(index)` checks if a detected Wi-Fi network is hidden. Hidden networks do not broadcast their SSID, making them less visible to users.

Use Purpose

The function is used to:

- **Identify hidden networks** that may not appear in standard scans.
- **Enable manual connections** to known hidden networks.
- **Improve network security** by detecting and analyzing hidden networks.

Arduino Syntax Use

```
bool hidden = WiFi.isHidden(index);
```

Arduino Syntax Explanation

1. **WiFi**: The built-in library used for managing Wi-Fi functions on the ESP32.
2. **isHidden()**: A function that returns whether a specific Wi-Fi network is hidden.
   - **Parameter index**: Refers to the network's position in the list.
   - **Return Value**: Returns `true` if the network is hidden, otherwise `false`.

Arduino Simple Code Example

```
#include <WiFi.h>

void setup() {
  Serial.begin(115200);

  int numberOfNetworks = WiFi.scanNetworks();
  Serial.println("Networks found:");

  for (int i = 0; i < numberOfNetworks; i++) {
```

```
  // Check if the network is hidden
  Serial.print("Network Name (SSID): ");
  Serial.print(WiFi.SSID(i));
  Serial.print(", Hidden: ");
  Serial.println(WiFi.isHidden(i) ? "Yes" : "No");
  }
}

void loop() {
  // Main code here
}
```

Notes

- Hidden networks are still detectable but require the correct SSID for connection.
- Hiding the SSID adds minimal security and should not be the sole security measure.

Warnings

- Hidden networks may require manual configuration to connect.
- Some Wi-Fi scanners may not detect all hidden networks.

Complete Real-Life Project Code for Wi-Fi Scan

Project Name: ESP32 Wi-Fi Network Scanner

Project Goal

- **Scan for available Wi-Fi networks** using the ESP32.
- **Display each network's SSID, signal strength, encryption type, and whether it is hidden.**
- **Provide a simple overview of the local network environment.**

Project Code
```
#include <WiFi.h>
```

```cpp
void setup() {
  Serial.begin(115200);
  Serial.println("Starting Wi-Fi scan...");

  // Perform a network scan
  int numberOfNetworks = WiFi.scanNetworks();
  Serial.print("Number of networks found: ");
  Serial.println(numberOfNetworks);

  // Display details for each network
  for (int i = 0; i < numberOfNetworks; i++) {
    Serial.print("Network Name (SSID): ");
    Serial.println(WiFi.SSID(i));

    Serial.print("Signal Strength (RSSI): ");
    Serial.println(WiFi.RSSI(i));

    Serial.print("Encryption Type: ");
    Serial.println(WiFi.encryptionType(i));

  }
}

void loop() {
  // Main code here
}
```

Save and Run

1. **Open the Arduino IDE** and create a new sketch.
2. **Copy the project code** above into the new sketch.
3. **Connect your ESP32** to your computer via USB.
4. **Configure the Arduino IDE**:
   - Go to **Tools > Board** and select **ESP32 Dev Module**.
   - Go to **Tools > Port** and choose the appropriate COM port.
5. **Upload the code** by clicking on the **Upload button**.

Check Output

1. **Open the Serial Monitor** in the Arduino IDE (Tools > Serial Monitor).
2. **Set the baud rate** to **115200**.
3. The Serial Monitor should display:
   - **Number of networks found**.
   - **Details for each network**, including SSID, RSSI, encryption type, and whether the network is hidden.

```
Starting Wi-Fi scan...
Number of networks found: 6
Network Name (SSID): H
Signal Strength (RSSI): -24
Encryption Type: 4
Network Name (SSID): MHome
Signal Strength (RSSI): -73
Encryption Type: 3
Network Name (SSID): Jeba
Signal Strength (RSSI): -91
Encryption Type: 4
Network Name (SSID): Principal House main
Signal Strength (RSSI): -92
```

This project demonstrates the basics of performing a **Wi-Fi Scan on ESP32**, allowing you to detect available networks and retrieve useful information about each one.

8.5. Wi-Fi Connect on ESP32

This guide will teach you how to **connect the ESP32 to a Wi-Fi network,** an essential skill for developing IoT projects that need internet access or communication with other devices on the same network. We will cover the basic functions needed to connect to a Wi-Fi network, check the connection status, handle connection errors, and a practical project example to demonstrate the process of **Wi-Fi Connect on ESP32**.

What is Wi-Fi Connect on ESP32?

Wi-Fi Connect on ESP32 allows the device to connect to an existing Wi-Fi network (Station Mode), enabling it to access the internet, communicate with cloud services, or interact with other devices on the network. This function is vital for IoT applications that require data transmission, remote monitoring, or online updates.

Syntax Table for Wi-Fi Connect Functions

Serial No.	Topic	Syntax	Simple Example
1	**Connect to Wi-Fi**	`WiFi.begin(ssid, password)`	`WiFi.begin("MySSID", "MyPassword");`
2	**Check Connection Status**	`WiFi.status()`	`if (WiFi.status() == WL_CONNECTED) { ... }`
3	**Reconnect to Wi-Fi**	`WiFi.reconnect()`	`WiFi.reconnect();`
4	**Disconnect from Wi-Fi**	`WiFi.disconnect()`	`WiFi.disconnect();`

5	**Get Local IP Address**	WiFi.localIP()	IPAddress ip = WiFi.localIP();

The table above summarizes the functions used to implement **Wi-Fi Connect on ESP32**, covering connecting, checking status, reconnecting, and retrieving network information.

1. Connecting to a Wi-Fi Network Using WiFi.begin(ssid, password)

What is WiFi.begin(ssid, password)?

WiFi.begin(ssid, password) is the function used to connect the ESP32 to a Wi-Fi network. It requires the network's SSID (name) and password for authentication.

Use Purpose

This function is used to:

- **Connect the ESP32 to a Wi-Fi network** for internet access.
- **Enable communication** with other devices on the network.
- **Provide a network interface** for remote monitoring or control.

Arduino Syntax Use
WiFi.begin(ssid, password);

Arduino Syntax Explanation

1. **WiFi**: Refers to the built-in Wi-Fi library for the ESP32, which provides functions for network management.
2. **begin()**: A function that initiates the connection to a specified Wi-Fi network.
   - **Parameters**:
     - ssid: The SSID (name) of the Wi-Fi network to connect to (string).

- password: The password for the network (string).
  - **Return Value**: The function does not directly return a value; the connection status should be checked using `WiFi.status()`.

Arduino Simple Code Example

```
#include <WiFi.h>

// Wi-Fi credentials
const char* ssid = "Your_SSID";         // Replace with
your network's SSID
const char* password = "Your_PASSWORD";  // Replace with
your network's password

void setup() {
  Serial.begin(115200);
  Serial.println("Connecting to Wi-Fi...");

  // Connect to Wi-Fi
  WiFi.begin(ssid, password);

  // Wait for the connection to establish
  while (WiFi.status() != WL_CONNECTED) {
    delay(500);
    Serial.print(".");
  }

  Serial.println("\nConnected to Wi-Fi!");
}
void loop() {
  // Main code here
}
```

Notes

- The SSID and password are case-sensitive.
- The ESP32 must be within the range of the Wi-Fi network for successful connection.

Warnings

- **Hardcoding credentials** may pose a security risk.
- **Incorrect SSID or password** will result in connection failure.

---

2. Checking Wi-Fi Connection Status Using WiFi.status()

What is WiFi.status()?

WiFi.status() checks the current connection status of the ESP32 and returns various status codes indicating whether the device is connected, connecting, or disconnected.

Use Purpose

The function is used to:

- **Verify whether the ESP32 is connected** before performing network tasks.
- **Monitor connection status** for error handling.

Arduino Syntax Use
WiFi.status();

Arduino Syntax Explanation

1. **WiFi**: Represents the Wi-Fi library used for managing Wi-Fi functionalities.
2. **status()**: A function that returns the connection status as an integer value. Possible return values include:
   - **WL_CONNECTED**: The ESP32 is connected to a Wi-Fi network.
   - **WL_DISCONNECTED**: The ESP32 is not connected to any network.

- WL_NO_SSID_AVAIL: The specified SSID is not available.
- WL_CONNECT_FAILED: The connection failed due to incorrect credentials.

Arduino Simple Code Example

```
#include <WiFi.h>

void setup() {
  Serial.begin(115200);
  WiFi.begin("Your_SSID", "Your_PASSWORD");

  // Check the connection status
  if (WiFi.status() == WL_CONNECTED) {
    Serial.println("Connected to Wi-Fi.");
  } else {
    Serial.println("Not connected to Wi-Fi.");
  }
}

void loop() {
  // Main code here
}
```

Notes

- Use WiFi.status() in loops to continuously monitor connection status.
- Helps in debugging connectivity issues.

Warnings

- **Intermittent network issues** may cause the status to change frequently.
- Implement retry mechanisms to handle connection failures gracefully.

3. Reconnecting to a Wi-Fi Network Using `WiFi.reconnect()`

What is `WiFi.reconnect()`?

`WiFi.reconnect()` attempts to reconnect the ESP32 to the last known Wi-Fi network. This can be useful if the connection was lost.

Use Purpose

This function is used to:

- **Re-establish a lost connection** without resetting the device.
- **Maintain network connectivity** for long-running tasks.

Arduino Syntax Use
`WiFi.reconnect();`

Arduino Syntax Explanation

1. `WiFi`: The library that provides Wi-Fi functionalities for the ESP32.
2. `reconnect()`: Attempts to reconnect the ESP32 to the last network it was connected to.
   - **Return Value**: The function does not return a value. Check the connection status with `WiFi.status()`.

Arduino Simple Code Example
```
#include <WiFi.h>
void setup() {
  Serial.begin(115200);
  WiFi.begin("Your_SSID", "Your_PASSWORD");

  // Try reconnecting if disconnected
  if (WiFi.status() != WL_CONNECTED) {
    WiFi.reconnect();
    Serial.println("Reconnecting to Wi-Fi...");
  } else {
    Serial.println("Already connected.");
  }
```

```
}

void loop() {
  // Main code here
}
```

Notes

- Use this function to recover from temporary network failures.
- Helps ensure a stable connection for critical tasks.

Warnings

- Reconnection may fail if the network is unavailable or credentials have changed.
- Use proper error handling to manage repeated reconnection attempts.

---

4. Disconnecting from Wi-Fi Using `WiFi.disconnect()`

What is `WiFi.disconnect()`?

`WiFi.disconnect()` disconnects the ESP32 from the current Wi-Fi network, freeing up network resources.

Use Purpose

The function is used to:

- **Switch to a different Wi-Fi network** without restarting the ESP32.
- **Reduce power consumption** by disconnecting from Wi-Fi when not needed.

Arduino Syntax Use
```
WiFi.disconnect();
```

Arduino Syntax Explanation

1. **WiFi**: Refers to the built-in Wi-Fi library for the ESP32.

2. **disconnect ()**: This function terminates the current Wi-Fi connection.
    - **Parameter (optional)**: You can pass `true` to turn off the Wi-Fi interface entirely.
    - **Return Value**: This function does not return a value. Check the status using `WiFi.status ()`.

Arduino Simple Code Example

```
#include <WiFi.h>

void setup() {
  Serial.begin(115200);

  // Disconnect from Wi-Fi
  WiFi.disconnect();
  Serial.println("Disconnected from Wi-Fi.");
}

void loop() {
  // Main code here
}
```

Notes

- Reconnect using `WiFi.begin()` if needed.
- Disconnecting saves power for battery-operated projects.

Warnings

- Disconnecting will end any active network communications.
- Ensure all network-dependent tasks are complete before disconnecting.

5. Retrieving the Local IP Address Using WiFi.localIP()

What is WiFi.localIP()?

WiFi.localIP() returns the IP address assigned to the ESP32 when it is connected to a network. This IP address is used to communicate with other devices on the same network.

Use Purpose

The function is used to:

- **Identify the ESP32's IP address** for network communication.
- **Debug network connectivity issues** by checking the assigned IP.
- **Set up servers or clients** using the local IP.

Arduino Syntax Use
```
IPAddress ip = WiFi.localIP();
```

Arduino Syntax Explanation

1. **WiFi**: Represents the Wi-Fi library that provides networking functionalities.
2. **localIP()**: Retrieves the local IP address assigned to the ESP32.
   o **Return Value**: Returns an IPAddress object containing the current local IP address.

Arduino Simple Code Example
```
#include <WiFi.h>

void setup() {
  Serial.begin(115200);
  WiFi.begin("Your_SSID", "Your_PASSWORD");

  while (WiFi.status() != WL_CONNECTED) {
    delay(500);
  }

  // Print the local IP address
  Serial.print("Local IP Address: ");
  Serial.println(WiFi.localIP());
}
```

```
void loop() {
  // Main code here
}
```

Notes

- The IP address is typically assigned by the network's DHCP server.
- Useful for applications like web servers or data logging.

Warnings

- If not connected to a network, `WiFi.localIP()` will return `0.0.0.0`.
- Avoid exposing the IP address in unsecured environments.

Complete Real-Life Project Code for Wi-Fi Connect

Project Name: ESP32 Wi-Fi Connection Monitor

Project Goal

- **Connect to a Wi-Fi network** using the ESP32.
- **Display the connection status and local IP address** on the Serial Monitor.
- **Reconnect if the connection is lost**.

Project Code

```
#include <WiFi.h>

// Wi-Fi credentials
const char* ssid = "Your_SSID";              // Replace with
your network's SSID
const char* password = "Your_PASSWORD";   // Replace with
your network's password

void setup() {
  Serial.begin(115200);
  Serial.println("Connecting to Wi-Fi...");
```

```
  // Connect to Wi-Fi
  WiFi.begin(ssid, password);

  // Wait for the connection to establish
  while (WiFi.status() != WL_CONNECTED) {
    delay(500);
    Serial.print(".");
  }

  Serial.println("\nConnected to Wi-Fi!");
  Serial.print("Local IP Address: ");
  Serial.println(WiFi.localIP());
}

void loop() {
  // Monitor the connection status
  if (WiFi.status() != WL_CONNECTED) {
    Serial.println("Connection lost. Reconnecting...");
    WiFi.reconnect();

    // Wait for reconnection
    while (WiFi.status() != WL_CONNECTED) {
      delay(500);
      Serial.print(".");
    }

    Serial.println("\nReconnected to Wi-Fi.");
    Serial.print("Local IP Address: ");
    Serial.println(WiFi.localIP());
  }

  delay(10000); // Check the connection status every 10
seconds
}
```

Save and Run

1. **Open the Arduino IDE** and create a new sketch.
2. **Copy the project code** above into the new sketch.
3. **Connect your ESP32** to your computer via USB.
4. **Configure the Arduino IDE**:
   o   Go to **Tools > Board** and select **ESP32 Dev Module**.
   o   Go to **Tools > Port** and choose the appropriate COM port.
5. **Upload the code** by clicking on the **Upload button**.

Check Output

1. **Open the Serial Monitor** in the Arduino IDE (Tools > Serial Monitor).
2. **Set the baud rate** to **115200**.
3. The Serial Monitor should display:
   o   **Connection progress** with dots until connected.
   o   **Connected status and local IP address**.
   o   **Reconnection status** if the connection is lost.

This project demonstrates the basics of **Wi-Fi Connect on ESP32**, including connecting to a network, checking connection status, and handling disconnections.

8.6 Wi-Fi Sleep Modes on ESP3

This guide will teach you about **Wi-Fi Sleep Modes on ESP32**, which are used to save power by reducing the Wi-Fi module's activity when it's not needed. Understanding and using sleep modes can help extend battery life in IoT projects, especially for devices running on limited power sources. We will cover different types of Wi-Fi sleep modes, their configurations, and a practical example demonstrating how to implement Wi-Fi sleep modes on the ESP32.

What are Wi-Fi Sleep Modes on ESP32?

Wi-Fi Sleep Modes on ESP32 are power-saving states that reduce the activity of the Wi-Fi module to conserve energy. These modes are especially useful for battery-operated devices and low-power IoT applications. There are three primary sleep modes available on the ESP32:

1. **Active Mode**: The default mode where Wi-Fi is fully operational.
2. **Modem Sleep**: Disables the Wi-Fi modem while keeping the CPU active.
3. **Light Sleep**: Keeps the CPU in a low-power state while disabling the Wi-Fi modem.
4. **Deep Sleep**: The most energy-efficient mode where both the CPU and Wi-Fi are powered down, but can be woken up by external events.

Syntax Table for Wi-Fi Sleep Modes

Se rial No.	Top ic	Syntax	Simple Example
1	**Ena ble Mo de m Sle ep**	`WiFi.setSleep(WIFI_PS_M IN_MODEM)`	`WiFi.setSleep(WIFI_PS_ MIN_MODEM);`
2	**Ena ble Lig ht Sle ep**	`esp_sleep_enable_timer_ wakeup(time_in_us)`	`esp_sleep_enable_timer _wakeup(5000000);`
3	**Ent er Dee p Sle ep**	`esp_deep_sleep_start()`	`esp_deep_sleep_start() ;`
4	**Dis able Sle ep Mo de**	`WiFi.setSleep(WIFI_PS_N ONE)`	`WiFi.setSleep(WIFI_PS_ NONE);`

This table provides an overview of functions used to configure and manage **Wi-Fi Sleep Modes on ESP32**, allowing you to optimize power consumption.

1. Enabling Modem Sleep Using
`WiFi.setSleep(WIFI_PS_MIN_MODEM)`

What is Modem Sleep?

Modem Sleep is a Wi-Fi sleep mode that disables the Wi-Fi modem while keeping the CPU active. This mode is suitable for tasks where the ESP32 needs to process data but doesn't need constant Wi-Fi connectivity.

Use Purpose

The function is used to:

- **Reduce power consumption** by turning off the Wi-Fi modem when not in use.
- **Keep the CPU active for processing tasks** while the Wi-Fi is disabled.
- **Extend battery life** in low-power applications.

Arduino Syntax Use
`WiFi.setSleep(WIFI_PS_MIN_MODEM);`

Arduino Syntax Explanation

1. `WiFi`: Represents the built-in Wi-Fi library for managing wireless connectivity on the ESP32.
2. `setSleep()`: A function that configures the Wi-Fi power-saving mode.
   - **Parameter**:
     - `WIFI_PS_MIN_MODEM`: Configures the ESP32 to use Modem Sleep mode, which turns off the Wi-Fi modem when not in use.
   - **Return Value**: The function does not return any value.

Arduino Simple Code Example

```
#include <WiFi.h>

void setup() {
  Serial.begin(115200);

  // Enable Modem Sleep mode
  WiFi.setSleep(WIFI_PS_MIN_MODEM);
  Serial.println("Modem Sleep mode enabled");
}

void loop() {
  // Main code here
}
```

Notes

- The CPU remains fully active in Modem Sleep mode.
- Suitable for applications where data processing is needed but not constant Wi-Fi connectivity.

Warnings

- Wi-Fi communication is disabled while in Modem Sleep.
- Ensure critical Wi-Fi tasks are completed before enabling Modem Sleep.

---

2. Enabling Light Sleep Using `esp_sleep_enable_timer_wakeup(time_in_us)`

What is Light Sleep?

Light Sleep reduces power consumption further than Modem Sleep by keeping the CPU in a low-power state while disabling the Wi-Fi modem. The ESP32 can wake up from Light Sleep using timers or external events.

Use Purpose

This function is used to:

- **Save more power** compared to Modem Sleep by putting the CPU in a low-power state.
- **Wake up from sleep based on timers or external events**.
- **Maintain some level of responsiveness** while saving energy.

Arduino Syntax Use

esp_sleep_enable_timer_wakeup(time_in_us);

Arduino Syntax Explanation

1. **esp_sleep_enable_timer_wakeup**(): Configures the ESP32 to wake up from Light Sleep after a specified period.
   - **Parameter**:
     - time_in_us: The duration in microseconds after which the ESP32 will wake up from Light Sleep.
   - **Return Value**: The function does not return any value.

Arduino Simple Code Example

```
#include <WiFi.h>
#include <esp_sleep.h>

void setup() {
  Serial.begin(115200);

  // Enable Light Sleep mode for 5 seconds
  esp_sleep_enable_timer_wakeup(5000000);
  Serial.println("Entering Light Sleep mode...");

  // Enter Light Sleep
  esp_light_sleep_start();
  Serial.println("Woke up from Light Sleep");
}
```

```
void loop() {
  // Main code here
}
```

Notes

- Light Sleep wakes up faster than Deep Sleep.
- The ESP32 can wake up using timers, touch, or other external events.

Warnings

- Wi-Fi connectivity is lost during Light Sleep.
- Light Sleep may not be suitable for real-time applications requiring immediate responses.

---

3. Entering Deep Sleep Using `esp_deep_sleep_start()`

What is Deep Sleep?

Deep Sleep is the most energy-efficient sleep mode for the ESP32. It powers down the CPU and Wi-Fi, leaving only the RTC (Real-Time Clock) active. The ESP32 can be woken up from Deep Sleep by timers, touch sensors, or external GPIO triggers.

Use Purpose

The function is used to:

- **Minimize power consumption** in battery-operated applications.
- **Extend battery life** for long-term deployments.
- **Wake up the ESP32 periodically** to perform specific tasks.

Arduino Syntax Use
```
esp_deep_sleep_start();
```

Arduino Syntax Explanation

1. **esp_deep_sleep_start()**: Puts the ESP32 into Deep Sleep mode, where the CPU and Wi-Fi are powered down.

- o **Return Value**: The function does not return any value, as the device will go into Deep Sleep immediately.

Arduino Simple Code Example

```
#include <esp_sleep.h>

void setup() {
  Serial.begin(115200);

  // Configure Deep Sleep for 10 seconds
  esp_sleep_enable_timer_wakeup(10000000);
  Serial.println("Entering Deep Sleep for 10 seconds...");

  // Enter Deep Sleep
  esp_deep_sleep_start();
}

void loop() {
  // This code will not be executed because the device is in
Deep Sleep
}
```

Notes

- Deep Sleep consumes the least power compared to other sleep modes.
- It is ideal for applications where the ESP32 performs periodic tasks.

Warnings

- The device's memory and state are lost in Deep Sleep.
- The ESP32 restarts when it wakes up from Deep Sleep.

---

4. Disabling Sleep Mode Using WiFi.setSleep(WIFI_PS_NONE)

What is Disabling Sleep Mode?

Disabling sleep mode ensures that the Wi-Fi module remains active at all times. This setting is useful for applications that require a constant and stable Wi-Fi connection.

Use Purpose

The function is used to:

- **Keep the Wi-Fi module active continuously** for real-time applications.
- **Ensure low latency** in network communication.
- **Disable power-saving features** when not needed.

Arduino Syntax Use
WiFi.setSleep(WIFI_PS_NONE);

Arduino Syntax Explanation

1. **WiFi**: The Wi-Fi library for the ESP32, managing wireless settings.
2. **setSleep()**: A function that disables all Wi-Fi power-saving modes.
   - **Parameter**:
     - WIFI_PS_NONE: Keeps the Wi-Fi module active without any sleep mode.
   - **Return Value**: This function does not return any value.

Arduino Simple Code Example

```
#include <WiFi.h>

void setup() {
  Serial.begin(115200);

  // Disable Wi-Fi Sleep mode
  WiFi.setSleep(WIFI_PS_NONE);
  Serial.println("Wi-Fi Sleep mode disabled");
}

void loop() {
  // Main code here
```

}

Notes

- Disabling sleep mode increases power consumption.
- Useful for applications requiring a constant network connection.

Warnings

- May significantly reduce battery life in portable devices.
- Ensure a reliable power source if sleep mode is disabled.

Complete Real-Life Project Code for Wi-Fi Sleep Modes

Project Name: ESP32 Battery Saver with Sleep Modes

Project Goal

- **Switch between different Wi-Fi sleep modes** to optimize power consumption.
- **Demonstrate Modem Sleep, Light Sleep, and Deep Sleep**.
- **Provide feedback** on the current sleep mode to the Serial Monitor.

Project Code

```
#include <WiFi.h>
#include <esp_sleep.h>

// Wi-Fi credentials
const char* ssid = "Your_SSID";          // Replace with
your network's SSID
const char* password = "Your_PASSWORD";   // Replace with
your network's password

void setup() {
  Serial.begin(115200);
  Serial.println("Connecting to Wi-Fi...");
```

```cpp
  // Connect to Wi-Fi
  WiFi.begin(ssid, password);
  while (WiFi.status() != WL_CONNECTED) {
    delay(500);
    Serial.print(".");
  }

  Serial.println("\nConnected to Wi-Fi!");

  // Example: Enable Modem Sleep for power saving
  WiFi.setSleep(WIFI_PS_MIN_MODEM);
  Serial.println("Modem Sleep mode enabled");

  // Example: Enter Light Sleep for 5 seconds
  esp_sleep_enable_timer_wakeup(5000000);
  Serial.println("Entering Light Sleep...");
  esp_light_sleep_start();
  Serial.println("Woke up from Light Sleep");

  // Example: Enter Deep Sleep for 10 seconds
  esp_sleep_enable_timer_wakeup(10000000);
  Serial.println("Entering Deep Sleep...");
  esp_deep_sleep_start();
}

void loop() {
  // No code needed for the loop in this example
}
```

Save and Run

1. **Open the Arduino IDE** and create a new sketch.
2. **Copy the project code** above into the new sketch.
3. **Connect your ESP32** to your computer via USB.
4. **Configure the Arduino IDE**:
   - ○ Go to **Tools > Board** and select **ESP32 Dev Module**.
   - ○ Go to **Tools > Port** and choose the appropriate COM port.
5. **Upload the code** by clicking on the **Upload button**.

Check Output

1. **Open the Serial Monitor** in the Arduino IDE (Tools > Serial Monitor).
2. **Set the baud rate** to **115200**.
3. The Serial Monitor should display:
   - ○ **Connection progress** with dots until connected.
   - ○ **Status messages** indicating the current sleep mode.
   - ○ **Wake-up messages** after Light Sleep and Deep Sleep.

This project demonstrates how to use **Wi-Fi Sleep Modes on ESP32** to optimize power consumption, making it suitable for battery-powered IoT devices.

8.7 Wi-Fi Smart Config on ESP32

Chapter Overview

This guide explains how to use **Wi-Fi Smart Config on ESP32** to configure Wi-Fi credentials easily. Smart Config is a method that allows users to set up their ESP32 Wi-Fi network without hardcoding the SSID and password in the code. The network credentials are sent from a smartphone or tablet, making it user-friendly for non-technical users or for devices that need frequent network changes. In this chapter, we will cover how to implement Smart Config, including a detailed explanation of the functions involved and a practical project to demonstrate **Wi-Fi Smart Config on ESP32**.

What is Wi-Fi Smart Config on ESP32?

Wi-Fi Smart Config on ESP32 allows you to configure network settings wirelessly using a smartphone. It enables the ESP32 to receive the Wi-Fi network SSID and password directly from a mobile app, such as the ESP-Touch app (available on iOS and Android), or other third-party apps supporting Smart Config. This feature simplifies the process of connecting ESP32 devices to different networks without modifying and uploading code.

Syntax Table for Wi-Fi Smart Config Functions

Serial No.	Topic	Syntax	Simple Example
1	**Start Smart Config**	WiFi.beginSmartConfig()	WiFi.beginSmartConfig();
2	**Check Smart Config Status**	WiFi.smartConfigDone()	if (WiFi.smartConfigDone()) { ... }
3	**Stop Smart Config**	WiFi.stopSmartConfig()	WiFi.stopSmartConfig();
4	**Get Smart Config Type**	WiFi.smartConfigType()	WiFi.smartConfigType(SC_TYPE_ESPTOUCH);
5	**Check Wi-Fi Connec**	WiFi.status()	if (WiFi.status() == WL_CONNECTED) { ... }

tion Status		

The table above lists the functions used for implementing **Wi-Fi Smart Config on ESP32**, including starting, checking status, stopping the process, and configuring Smart Config types.

1. Starting Smart Config Using `WiFi.beginSmartConfig()`

What is `WiFi.beginSmartConfig()`?

`WiFi.beginSmartConfig()` initiates the Smart Config process, allowing the ESP32 to receive the SSID and password from a smartphone. The Smart Config app on a smartphone transmits the network credentials to the ESP32 over the air.

Use Purpose

This function is used to:

- **Enable the Smart Config mode** on the ESP32 to receive network credentials.
- **Set up Wi-Fi credentials without hardcoding** them in the code.
- **Allow easy network configuration** in situations where the device is moved to different networks.

Arduino Syntax Use
`WiFi.beginSmartConfig();`

Arduino Syntax Explanation

1. `WiFi`: Refers to the built-in Wi-Fi library for the ESP32, which provides functions for managing network settings.
2. `beginSmartConfig()`: This function starts the Smart Config mode on the ESP32.

- What it does: Puts the ESP32 into Smart Config listening mode, where it waits to receive the Wi-Fi SSID and password from a smartphone. The smartphone app transmits these credentials using broadcast packets.
- How it works:
  - The Smart Config app uses the local network to send encoded SSID and password information.
  - The ESP32 listens for these packets and decodes them to get the network details.
- Supported Types: The default Smart Config type is SC_TYPE_ESPTOUCH, which is supported by the ESP-Touch app.
3. Return Value: This function does not return any value. To determine if the Smart Config process has completed, you can use WiFi.smartConfigDone().

Arduino Simple Code Example

```cpp
#include <WiFi.h>

void setup() {
  Serial.begin(115200);
  Serial.println("Starting Smart Config...");

  // Start Smart Config
  WiFi.beginSmartConfig();

  // Wait for Smart Config to complete
  while (!WiFi.smartConfigDone()) {
    delay(500);
    Serial.print(".");
  }

  Serial.println("\nSmart Config Done!");
}

void loop() {
  // Main code here
}
```

Notes

- Ensure that the ESP-Touch app or another Smart Config app is installed on the smartphone.
- Make sure the smartphone and ESP32 are connected to the same local network during the configuration.

Warnings

- Smart Config may take a few seconds to complete, depending on network conditions.
- Avoid using Smart Config in noisy network environments to prevent data packet loss.

---

2. Checking Smart Config Status Using WiFi.smartConfigDone()

What is WiFi.smartConfigDone()?

WiFi.smartConfigDone() checks if the Smart Config process has successfully completed. It returns true if the ESP32 has received the Wi-Fi credentials from the smartphone.

Use Purpose

This function is used to:

- **Verify if the Smart Config process is finished**.
- **Move to the next steps** once the Wi-Fi credentials are successfully received.
- **Provide feedback to the user** indicating the configuration status.

Arduino Syntax Use
WiFi.smartConfigDone();

Arduino Syntax Explanation

1. **WiFi**: Represents the built-in Wi-Fi library used for managing Smart Config and other network functions.

2. **smartConfigDone ()**: This function checks if the Smart Config process has completed.
   - o **Return Value**: Returns true if the Smart Config process has successfully received the network credentials; otherwise, returns false.
   - o **Usage**: Typically used in a loop to wait for the Smart Config process to complete before proceeding.

Arduino Simple Code Example

```
#include <WiFi.h>

void setup() {
  Serial.begin(115200);
  WiFi.beginSmartConfig();

  // Wait for Smart Config to complete
  while (!WiFi.smartConfigDone()) {
    delay(500);
    Serial.print(".");
  }

  Serial.println("\nSmart Config completed successfully!");
}

void loop() {
  // Main code here
}
```

Notes

- This function should be called frequently (e.g., inside a loop) to continuously check the status.
- Once WiFi.smartConfigDone() returns true, you can proceed to connect the ESP32 to the received network.

Warnings

- If WiFi.smartConfigDone() is not used properly, the program may hang waiting for the configuration to complete.
- Ensure that the Smart Config app is sending the network credentials before checking the status.

3. Stopping Smart Config Using WiFi.stopSmartConfig()

What is WiFi.stopSmartConfig()?

WiFi.stopSmartConfig() stops the Smart Config process on the ESP32. This function can be used to end the Smart Config mode manually if needed.

Use Purpose

The function is used to:

- **Manually stop the Smart Config process** if it is no longer needed.
- **Terminate the listening mode** after a certain timeout.
- **Free up resources** once the network credentials are received.

Arduino Syntax Use

WiFi.stopSmartConfig();

Arduino Syntax Explanation

1. **WiFi**: Refers to the built-in Wi-Fi library on the ESP32.
2. **stopSmartConfig()**: Ends the Smart Config process.
   - **What it does**: Stops the Smart Config listening mode, which is useful if you want to terminate the process after a timeout or if the configuration has been completed.
   - **Usage**: Use this function when you want to stop Smart Config manually.
3. **Return Value**: This function does not return any value.

Arduino Simple Code Example

```
#include <WiFi.h>

void setup() {
  Serial.begin(115200);
  WiFi.beginSmartConfig();

  unsigned long startTime = millis();

  // Wait for Smart Config to complete with a timeout of 30
seconds
  while (!WiFi.smartConfigDone() && millis() - startTime <
30000) {
    delay(500);
    Serial.print(".");
  }

  if (WiFi.smartConfigDone()) {
    Serial.println("\nSmart Config completed
successfully!");
  } else {
    // Stop Smart Config if it doesn't complete in 30
seconds
    WiFi.stopSmartConfig();
    Serial.println("\nSmart Config timed out.");
  }
}

void loop() {
  // Main code here
}
```

Notes

- It is useful to stop Smart Config after a certain timeout to avoid hanging the system.
- Make sure the Smart Config process is stopped when no longer needed.

Warnings

- If you stop Smart Config before it completes, the ESP32 will not receive the Wi-Fi credentials.
- Use proper error handling to manage unsuccessful Smart Config attempts.

---

4. Configuring Smart Config Type Using WiFi.smartConfigType()

What is WiFi.smartConfigType()?

WiFi.smartConfigType() allows you to specify the type of Smart Config method to use. The common types are SC_TYPE_ESPTOUCH and SC_TYPE_AIRKISS.

Use Purpose

This function is used to:

- **Set the type of Smart Config** method for the configuration process.
- **Ensure compatibility with the specific Smart Config app** being used.
- **Switch between different Smart Config protocols** as needed.

Arduino Syntax Use

WiFi.smartConfigType(SC_TYPE_ESPTOUCH);

Arduino Syntax Explanation

1. **WiFi**: Represents the built-in Wi-Fi library used for managing network settings on the ESP32.
2. **smartConfigType()**: Configures the type of Smart Config method to use.
   - **Parameter**:
     - SC_TYPE_ESPTOUCH: Uses the ESP-Touch protocol (default).
     - SC_TYPE_AIRKISS: Uses the AirKiss protocol.

- o **Usage**: Set the Smart Config type before starting the process with `WiFi.beginSmartConfig()`.
3. **Return Value**: This function does not return any value.

Arduino Simple Code Example

```
#include <WiFi.h>

void setup() {
  Serial.begin(115200);

  // Set the Smart Config type to ESP-Touch
  WiFi.smartConfigType(SC_TYPE_ESPTOUCH);
  Serial.println("Smart Config Type set to ESP-Touch");

  // Start Smart Config
  WiFi.beginSmartConfig();

  // Wait for Smart Config to complete
  while (!WiFi.smartConfigDone()) {
    delay(500);
    Serial.print(".");
  }

  Serial.println("\nSmart Config completed successfully!");
}

void loop() {
  // Main code here
}
```

Notes

- SC_TYPE_ESPTOUCH is commonly used with the ESP-Touch app.
- You can use SC_TYPE_AIRKISS if you need compatibility with WeChat's AirKiss.

Warnings

- Ensure that the selected Smart Config type matches the app being used.
- The wrong configuration type may cause Smart Config to fail.

Complete Real-Life Project Code for Wi-Fi Smart Config

Project Name: ESP32 Smart Config Wi-Fi Setup

Project Goal

- **Use Smart Config to set up the Wi-Fi connection** on the ESP32.
- **Provide feedback during the Smart Config process.**
- **Display the local IP address after connecting to the network.**

Project Code

```
#include <WiFi.h>

void setup() {
  Serial.begin(115200);
  Serial.println("Starting Smart Config...");

  // Start Smart Config
  WiFi.beginSmartConfig();

  // Wait for Smart Config to complete
  while (!WiFi.smartConfigDone()) {
    delay(500);
    Serial.print(".");
  }

  Serial.println("\nSmart Config completed successfully!");

  // Wait for Wi-Fi connection
  while (WiFi.status() != WL_CONNECTED) {
    delay(500);
    Serial.print(".");
```

```
  }

  Serial.println("¥nConnected to Wi-Fi!");
  Serial.print("Local IP Address: ");
  Serial.println(WiFi.localIP());
}

void loop() {
  // Main code here
}
```

Save and Run

1. **Open the Arduino IDE** and create a new sketch.
2. **Copy the project code** above into the new sketch.
3. **Connect your ESP32** to your computer via USB.
4. **Configure the Arduino IDE**:
   - Go to **Tools > Board** and select **ESP32 Dev Module**.
   - Go to **Tools > Port** and choose the appropriate COM port.
5. **Upload the code** by clicking on the **Upload button**.

Check Output

1. **Open the Serial Monitor** in the Arduino IDE (Tools > Serial Monitor).
2. **Set the baud rate** to **115200**.
3. **Use the ESP-Touch app** or another Smart Config app to send the Wi-Fi credentials.
4. The Serial Monitor should display:
   - **Progress dots for Smart Config.**
   - **Messages indicating successful configuration.**
   - **Local IP address** after connecting to the network.

```
Starting Smart Config...
.................................................
Smart Config completed successfully!

Connected to Wi-Fi!
Local IP Address: 192.168.0.103
```

☑ Autoscroll ☐ Show timestamp   Newline   ∨   115200 baud ∨

This project demonstrates how to implement **Wi-Fi Smart Config on ESP32**, allowing for easy network setup and configuration using a smartphone.

8.9 Wi-Fi SoftAP with Web Server on ESP32

This guide will teach you how to set up **Wi-Fi SoftAP with Web Server on ESP32**, which allows the ESP32 to create its own Wi-Fi network (SoftAP) and host a web server for controlling devices or displaying information. This configuration is perfect for IoT projects that require a local network without needing an external router. We will cover setting up the SoftAP, creating a simple web server, and the essential functions to implement this configuration.

What is Wi-Fi SoftAP with Web Server on ESP32?

Wi-Fi SoftAP with Web Server on ESP32 allows the ESP32 to create its own Wi-Fi network (Soft Access Point), which other devices can connect to. Once connected, users can access a web server hosted on the ESP32 to interact with it through a web browser. This setup is ideal for scenarios where no external Wi-Fi network is available or when a private local network is needed.

Syntax Table for Wi-Fi SoftAP with Web Server Functions

Serial No.	Topic	Syntax	Simple Example
1	**Set Up SoftAP**	`WiFi.softAP(ssid, password)`	`WiFi.softAP("MyESP32AP", "MyPassword123");`
2	**Get SoftAP IP Address**	`WiFi.softAPIP()`	`IPAddress apIP = WiFi.softAPIP();`
3	**Set Up Web Server**	`server.begin()`	`server.begin();`
4	**Handle Client Requests**	`server.handleClient()`	`server.handleClient();`
5	**Respond to HTTP Requests**	`server.on(path, HTTP_GET, function)`	`server.on("/", HTTP_GET, handleRoot);`

This table summarizes the primary functions needed to set up a **Wi-Fi SoftAP with Web Server on ESP32**, making it easier to create a self-hosted network and serve web pages.

1. Setting Up SoftAP Using `WiFi.softAP(ssid, password)`

What is `WiFi.softAP(ssid, password)`?

`WiFi.softAP(ssid, password)` is used to configure the ESP32 as an access point, allowing it to create its own Wi-Fi network with the given SSID (network name) and password. Other devices can connect to this network to communicate directly with the ESP32.

Use Purpose

This function is used to:

- **Create a private Wi-Fi network** that devices can connect to without an external router.
- **Allow direct communication** with the ESP32 over a local network.
- **Host local web servers** for controlling devices or displaying data.

Arduino Syntax Use
`WiFi.softAP(ssid, password);`

Arduino Syntax Explanation

1. `WiFi`: Refers to the built-in Wi-Fi library for the ESP32, which provides functions for managing both Station and Access Point modes.
2. `softAP()`: This function configures the ESP32 to create a Soft Access Point (SoftAP).
   - **Parameters**:
     - `ssid`: The SSID (network name) for the Wi-Fi network.
       - **Data Type**: `const char*` (a string in C++)
       - **Usage**: Specifies the name that devices will see when they search for Wi-Fi networks.
     - `password`: The password for the network.
       - **Data Type**: `const char*` (a string in C++)

- **Usage**: Provides security to prevent unauthorized connections. It must be at least 8 characters long.
  - ○ **Return Value**: This function does not return a value. To verify the setup, you can check the IP address using `WiFi.softAPIP()`.

Arduino Simple Code Example

```
#include <WiFi.h>

// Access Point credentials
const char* ssid = "MyESP32AP";          // Network name
const char* password = "MyPassword123";  // Network password

void setup() {
  Serial.begin(115200);

  // Set up the access point
  if (WiFi.softAP(ssid, password)) {
    Serial.println("Access Point Created");
    Serial.print("AP IP address: ");
    Serial.println(WiFi.softAPIP());
  } else {
    Serial.println("Failed to create Access Point");
  }
}

void loop() {
  // Main code here
}
```

Notes

- The SSID and password should be unique and secure to avoid conflicts.
- The default IP address for the access point is 192.168.4.1.

Warnings

- Using simple or weak passwords may allow unauthorized access.

- Be cautious when using open networks (no password), as they pose a security risk.

---

2. Getting the SoftAP IP Address Using WiFi.softAPIP()

What is WiFi.softAPIP()?

WiFi.softAPIP() retrieves the IP address assigned to the ESP32's Soft Access Point. This IP address is used by connected devices to access the web server hosted on the ESP32.

Use Purpose

The function is used to:

- **Identify the IP address** for clients to connect to the ESP32.
- **Set up web servers** that can be accessed by other devices on the same network.
- **Debug or verify the network configuration**.

Arduino Syntax Use
IPAddress apIP = WiFi.softAPIP();

Arduino Syntax Explanation

1. **WiFi**: Refers to the built-in Wi-Fi library that provides various networking functions.
2. **softAPIP()**: This function returns the IP address assigned to the ESP32's Soft Access Point.
   - **Return Value**: Returns an IPAddress object representing the IP address. By default, the IP address is 192.168.4.1 unless manually configured using WiFi.softAPConfig().

Arduino Simple Code Example

```
#include <WiFi.h>

void setup() {
  Serial.begin(115200);

  // Create a Soft Access Point
  WiFi.softAP("MyESP32AP", "MyPassword123");

  // Print the SoftAP IP address
  Serial.print("Access Point IP Address: ");
  Serial.println(WiFi.softAPIP());
}

void loop() {
  // Main code here
}
```

Notes

- You can customize the IP address using the WiFi.softAPConfig() function if needed.
- Knowing the IP address is crucial for accessing any services hosted on the ESP32.

Warnings

- Be sure not to use the same IP address as your primary network to avoid conflicts.
- Clients connected to the SoftAP should use the displayed IP address to communicate with the ESP32.

3. Setting Up a Web Server Using `server.begin()`

What is `server.begin()`?

`server.begin()` starts the web server on the ESP32, allowing it to handle incoming HTTP requests from clients connected to the SoftAP.

Use Purpose

This function is used to:

- **Initialize the web server** on the ESP32.
- **Listen for incoming requests** from clients.
- **Enable hosting of web pages or control interfaces**.

Arduino Syntax Use
`server.begin();`

Arduino Syntax Explanation

1. `server`: Refers to an instance of the `WebServer` class, which provides methods for setting up and managing a web server.
2. `begin()`: A function that starts the web server.
   - **What it does**: Makes the web server listen for incoming HTTP requests on the specified port (default is port 80).
   - **Usage**: Must be called after creating a `WebServer` instance.
3. **Return Value**: This function does not return any value.

Arduino Simple Code Example
```
#include <WiFi.h>
#include <WebServer.h>

// Create a WebServer object on port 80
WebServer server(80);

void setup() {
  Serial.begin(115200);
  WiFi.softAP("MyESP32AP", "MyPassword123");
```

```
  // Start the web server
  server.begin();
  Serial.println("Web server started");
}

void loop() {
  // Handle client requests
  server.handleClient();
}
```

Notes

- You need to set up request handling functions using server.on() before starting the server.
- The default port for the web server is 80, but it can be changed when creating the WebServer instance.

Warnings

- Ensure the server is properly set up to handle various HTTP requests.
- Starting the server without proper request handling may lead to unresponsive behavior.

---

4. Handling Client Requests Using server.handleClient()

What is server.handleClient()?

server.handleClient() processes incoming HTTP requests from connected clients and triggers the appropriate response functions.

Use Purpose

The function is used to:

- **Listen for incoming client requests.**
- **Trigger response functions** when specific endpoints are accessed.
- **Continuously check for new requests** in the main loop.

Arduino Syntax Use

```
server.handleClient();
```

Arduino Syntax Explanation

1. **server**: Represents the web server instance used to manage HTTP requests.
2. **handleClient()**: This function checks for new incoming client requests and calls the appropriate response function based on the requested URL.
   - **Usage**: Should be called frequently, typically inside the loop(), to continuously handle client requests.
3. **Return Value**: This function does not return any value.

Arduino Simple Code Example

```
#include <WiFi.h>
#include <WebServer.h>

WebServer server(80);

void setup() {
  Serial.begin(115200);
  WiFi.softAP("MyESP32AP", "MyPassword123");

  // Handle root URL request
  server.on("/", HTTP_GET, []() {
    server.send(200, "text/plain", "Hello, you are connected
to ESP32!");
  });

  // Start the server
  server.begin();
}

void loop() {
  // Handle incoming client requests
  server.handleClient();
}
```

Notes

- The function must be called frequently to ensure timely responses to client requests.
- Proper request handling improves user experience and server stability.

Warnings

- Failing to call `server.handleClient()` will result in unhandled requests.
- Always ensure the web server is correctly set up to handle different routes.

---

5. Responding to HTTP Requests Using `server.on(path, HTTP_GET, function)`

What is `server.on(path, HTTP_GET, function)`?

`server.on(path, HTTP_GET, function)` sets up a handler for HTTP requests to a specific URL path, allowing you to define custom responses for different endpoints.

Use Purpose

This function is used to:

- **Specify which function to execute** when a particular URL is accessed.
- **Define custom responses** for various endpoints.
- **Create dynamic web pages** that provide feedback or control.

Arduino Syntax Use
`server.on(path, HTTP_GET, function);`

Arduino Syntax Explanation

1. **server**: Represents the web server instance used for managing HTTP requests.
2. **on()**: Configures a handler for a specific URL path and HTTP method.
   - **Parameters**:

- path: The URL path (e.g., "/") that the server should listen for.
  - **Data Type**: const char* (string in C++)
- HTTP_GET: Specifies the HTTP method. Other methods include HTTP_POST, HTTP_PUT, etc.
- function: The callback function to execute when the specified path is accessed.
  - **Usage**: Defines how the server should respond to the request.
  - ○ **Return Value**: This function does not return any value.

Arduino Simple Code Example

```cpp
#include <WiFi.h>
#include <WebServer.h>

WebServer server(80);

void handleRoot() {
  server.send(200, "text/html", "<h1>Welcome to ESP32 Web Server</h1>");
}

void setup() {
  Serial.begin(115200);
  WiFi.softAP("MyESP32AP", "MyPassword123");

  // Handle requests to the root URL
  server.on("/", HTTP_GET, handleRoot);

  // Start the web server
  server.begin();
  Serial.println("Web server started");
}

void loop() {
  // Handle client requests
  server.handleClient();
```

}

Notes

- Multiple handlers can be set up for different URLs.
- Properly managing the server's response improves client interaction.

Warnings

- Make sure the server can handle requests efficiently to avoid delays.
- Ensure security measures are in place to prevent unauthorized access.

Complete Real-Life Project Code for Wi-Fi SoftAP with Web Server

Project Name: ESP32 Basic Control Interface

Project Goal

- **Create a SoftAP with a web server** to host a basic control interface.
- **Respond to HTTP requests** to control an LED.
- **Provide feedback on the LED's current state**.

Project Code

```
#include <WiFi.h>
#include <WebServer.h>

// Web server running on port 80
WebServer server(80);

// Access Point credentials
const char* ssid = "MyESP32AP";
const char* password = "MyPassword123";

// LED pin
```

```
const int ledPin = 2;

void handleRoot() {
  String html = "<h1>ESP32 Web Server</h1><p><a
href=¥"/on¥"><button>Turn ON</button></a></p><p><a
href=¥"/off¥"><button>Turn OFF</button></a></p>";
  server.send(200, "text/html", html);
}

void handleLEDOn() {
  digitalWrite(ledPin, HIGH);
  server.send(200, "text/plain", "LED is ON");
}

void handleLEDOff() {
  digitalWrite(ledPin, LOW);
  server.send(200, "text/plain", "LED is OFF");
}

void setup() {
  // Start serial monitor
  Serial.begin(115200);

  // Initialize LED pin
  pinMode(ledPin, OUTPUT);

  // Set up the SoftAP
  WiFi.softAP(ssid, password);

  // Set up web server routes
  server.on("/", HTTP_GET, handleRoot);
  server.on("/on", HTTP_GET, handleLEDOn);
  server.on("/off", HTTP_GET, handleLEDOff);

  // Start the web server
  server.begin();
  Serial.println("Web server started");
}
```

```
void loop() {
  // Handle client requests
  server.handleClient();
}
```

Save and Run

1. **Open the Arduino IDE** and create a new sketch.
2. **Copy the project code** above into the new sketch.
3. **Connect your ESP32** to your computer via USB.
4. **Configure the Arduino IDE**:
   - Go to **Tools > Board** and select **ESP32 Dev Module**.
   - Go to **Tools > Port** and choose the appropriate COM port.
5. **Upload the code** by clicking on the **Upload button**.

Check Output

1. **Open the Serial Monitor** in the Arduino IDE (Tools > Serial Monitor).
2. **Set the baud rate** to **115200**.
3. **Connect a device to the ESP32's SoftAP network**.
4. **Open a web browser** and go to http://192.168.4.1/.
5. **Control the LED** using the "Turn ON" and "Turn OFF" buttons.

ESP32 Web Server

Turn ON

Turn OFF

This project demonstrates how to set up a **Wi-Fi SoftAP with Web Server on ESP32**, allowing you to host a local network and provide a control interface for devices connected to the SoftAP.

Project With ESP32 WIFI

1 .Project Name: ESP32 Multi-Mode Network Manager

Project Overview

This project demonstrates how to use multiple networking capabilities on the ESP32, including **Station Mode (STA)**, **Access Point Mode (AP)**, **Station + Access Point Mode (STA+AP)**, **Wi-Fi Scan**, **Wi-Fi Smart Config**, and **Wi-Fi SoftAP with Web Server**. The goal is to create an all-in-one network management solution where the ESP32 can:

- **Connect to an existing Wi-Fi network** (Station Mode).
- **Create its own Wi-Fi network** (Access Point Mode).
- **Combine STA and AP modes for dual functionality.**
- **Scan for available networks** and display them.
- **Use Smart Config to configure network settings** wirelessly.
- **Host a web server in AP mode** to control the device or monitor status.

The project provides an interactive web interface for users to switch between modes, scan for networks, configure settings, and control an LED.

Project Goals

- **Provide multiple network modes for flexible connectivity.**
- **Host a web server accessible through AP mode for configuration and control.**
- **Scan and display available Wi-Fi networks.**
- **Enable Wi-Fi Smart Config for easy network configuration.**
- **Allow switching between Station Mode, Access Point Mode, and STA+AP Mode.**
- **Control an LED based on user commands via the web server.**

Project Components

1. **Station Mode (STA)**: The ESP32 connects to an existing Wi-Fi network to access the internet or communicate with other network devices.
2. **Access Point Mode (AP)**: The ESP32 creates its own Wi-Fi network for other devices to connect to directly.
3. **STA + AP Mode**: The ESP32 simultaneously connects to an existing Wi-Fi network and creates its own access point.
4. **Wi-Fi Scan**: Scans for available networks and displays them on the web interface.
5. **Wi-Fi Smart Config**: Configures the network settings wirelessly using a smartphone.
6. **Wi-Fi SoftAP with Web Server**: Hosts a web server in AP mode for configuration and device control.

Project Code

```
#include <WiFi.h>
#include <WebServer.h>

// Web server running on port 80
WebServer server(80);

// Access Point credentials
const char* apSSID = "ESP32_AP";
const char* apPassword = "12345678";

// Station Mode credentials (default)
const char* staSSID = "Your_SSID";
const char* staPassword = "Your_PASSWORD";

// LED pin
const int ledPin = 2;

// Network mode flags
bool isStationMode = false;
```

```cpp
bool isAccessPointMode = true; // Start in AP mode by
default

// Function to handle requests to root URL
void handleRoot() {
  String html = "<h1>ESP32 Multi-Mode Network Manager</h1>"
                "<p>Mode: " + String(isStationMode ?
"Station" : "Access Point") + "</p>"
                "<p><a href=¥"/sta¥"><button>Switch to
Station Mode</button></a></p>"
                "<p><a href=¥"/ap¥"><button>Switch to Access
Point Mode</button></a></p>"
                "<p><a href=¥"/staap¥"><button>Switch to
STA+AP Mode</button></a></p>"
                "<p><a href=¥"/scan¥"><button>Scan for
Networks</button></a></p>"
                "<p><a href=¥"/smartconfig¥"><button>Start
Smart Config</button></a></p>"
                "<p><a href=¥"/on¥"><button>Turn LED
ON</button></a></p>"
                "<p><a href=¥"/off¥"><button>Turn LED
OFF</button></a></p>";
  server.send(200, "text/html", html);
}

// Function to switch to Station Mode
void handleStationMode() {
  isStationMode = true;
  isAccessPointMode = false;
  WiFi.mode(WIFI_STA);
  WiFi.begin(staSSID, staPassword);
  server.send(200, "text/plain", "Switched to Station
Mode");
}

// Function to switch to Access Point Mode
void handleAccessPointMode() {
  isStationMode = false;
  isAccessPointMode = true;
```

```cpp
  WiFi.mode(WIFI_AP);
  WiFi.softAP(apSSID, apPassword);
  server.send(200, "text/plain", "Switched to Access Point
Mode");
}

// Function to switch to STA+AP Mode
void handleStationAccessPointMode() {
  isStationMode = true;
  isAccessPointMode = true;
  WiFi.mode(WIFI_AP_STA);
  WiFi.begin(staSSID, staPassword);
  WiFi.softAP(apSSID, apPassword);
  server.send(200, "text/plain", "Switched to STA+AP Mode");
}

// Function to scan for available networks
void handleScanNetworks() {
  int n = WiFi.scanNetworks();
  String networks = "<h1>Available Networks</h1>";
  for (int i = 0; i < n; ++i) {
    networks += "<p>" + String(WiFi.SSID(i)) + " (" +
String(WiFi.RSSI(i)) + " dBm)</p>";
  }
  server.send(200, "text/html", networks);
}

// Function to start Smart Config
void handleSmartConfig() {
  WiFi.beginSmartConfig();
  server.send(200, "text/plain", "Started Smart Config.
Please use the ESP-Touch app to configure.");
  while (!WiFi.smartConfigDone()) {
    delay(500);
    Serial.print(".");
  }
  Serial.println("\nSmart Config completed.");
}
```

```
// Function to handle LED ON command
void handleLEDOn() {
  digitalWrite(ledPin, HIGH);
  server.send(200, "text/plain", "LED is ON");
}

// Function to handle LED OFF command
void handleLEDOff() {
  digitalWrite(ledPin, LOW);
  server.send(200, "text/plain", "LED is OFF");
}

void setup() {
  Serial.begin(115200);

  // Initialize LED pin
  pinMode(ledPin, OUTPUT);

  // Set up web server routes
  server.on("/", handleRoot);
  server.on("/sta", handleStationMode);
  server.on("/ap", handleAccessPointMode);
  server.on("/staap", handleStationAccessPointMode);
  server.on("/scan", handleScanNetworks);
  server.on("/smartconfig", handleSmartConfig);
  server.on("/on", handleLEDOn);
  server.on("/off", handleLEDOff);

  // Start in Access Point Mode by default
  WiFi.softAP(apSSID, apPassword);
  server.begin();
  Serial.println("Web server started");
}

void loop() {
  // Handle incoming client requests
  server.handleClient();
}
```

Save and Run

1. **Open the Arduino IDE** and create a new sketch.
2. **Copy the project code** above into the new sketch.
3. **Connect your ESP32** to your computer via USB.
4. **Configure the Arduino IDE**:
   - Go to **Tools > Board** and select **ESP32 Dev Module**.
   - Go to **Tools > Port** and choose the appropriate COM port.
5. **Upload the code** by clicking on the **Upload button**.

Check Output

1. **Open the Serial Monitor** in the Arduino IDE (Tools > Serial Monitor).
2. **Set the baud rate** to **115200**.
3. **Connect a device to the ESP32's Access Point** with SSID "ESP32_AP" and password "12345678".
4. **Open a web browser and go to** http://192.168.4.1/.
5. **Use the web interface to switch between modes, scan networks, start Smart Config, and control the LED.**

ESP32 Multi-Mode Network Manager

Mode: Access Point

Switch to Station Mode

Switch to Access Point Mode

Switch to STA+AP Mode

Scan for Networks

Start Smart Config

Turn LED ON

Turn LED OFF

Project Summary

This project demonstrates how to implement various networking functionalities on the ESP32, including:

- **Station Mode** for connecting to existing networks.
- **Access Point Mode** for creating a private Wi-Fi network.
- **STA + AP Mode** for simultaneous network access and hosting.
- **Wi-Fi Scan** to detect available networks.
- **Smart Config** to configure Wi-Fi settings wirelessly.
- **Web server functionalities** for remote control and configuration.

The **ESP32 Multi-Mode Network Manager** serves as a comprehensive demonstration of the ESP32's networking capabilities, suitable for IoT applications requiring flexible and dynamic network configurations.

2. Project: ESP32 IoT Weather Station: Combining Wi-Fi Modes, Web Server, and Sensor Data

Project Overview

This project will guide you through building an **ESP32 IoT Weather Station** that uses various Wi-Fi modes (Station Mode, Access Point Mode, STA+AP), a web server, and a sensor (such as a DHT11 or DHT22 for temperature and humidity) to collect and display weather data. The ESP32 will:

- **Connect to an existing Wi-Fi network** in Station Mode to send data to cloud services.
- **Create its own Wi-Fi network** in Access Point Mode, allowing direct connection and local data access.
- **Combine STA+AP Mode** to provide simultaneous network access and local hosting.
- **Host a web server to display weather data.**
- **Scan for networks and configure settings using Smart Config.**
- **Provide a web-based interface for monitoring sensor data** and controlling the device.

Project Goals

- **Read temperature and humidity data** using a DHT11 or DHT22 sensor.
- **Provide multiple network connection modes** for flexibility.
- **Display weather data on a web server** hosted on the ESP32.
- **Allow users to connect directly to the ESP32 in AP mode** to view data.
- **Implement STA+AP mode for simultaneous local and internet access.**
- **Use Smart Config for easy network setup.**
- **Offer a web-based interface** to control and monitor the device.

Components Required

- **ESP32 development board**
- **DHT11 or DHT22 temperature and humidity sensor**
- **Resistor (10kΩ) for DHT sensor**
- **Jumper wires and breadboard**
- **Arduino IDE** with ESP32 libraries installed

Circuit Diagram

1. **DHT Sensor Connections**:
   - **VCC** to **3.3V** on ESP32
   - **GND** to **GND** on ESP32
   - **DATA** to **GPIO 4** on ESP32 (or another GPIO pin)
2. **Resistor (10kΩ)** between **VCC and DATA** pin of the DHT sensor.

Project Code

```
#include <WiFi.h>
#include <WebServer.h>
#include <DHT.h>

// Define DHT sensor type and pin
#define DHTTYPE DHT22 // Change to DHT11 if using DHT11
sensor
#define DHTPIN 4      // Pin where the DHT sensor is
connected
#define ledPin 2

DHT dht(DHTPIN, DHTTYPE);

// Web server running on port 80
WebServer server(80);
```

```cpp
// Access Point credentials
const char* apSSID = "ESP32_WeatherStation";
const char* apPassword = "12345678";

// Station Mode credentials (default)
const char* staSSID = "Your_SSID";
const char* staPassword = "Your_PASSWORD";

// Network mode flags
bool isStationMode = false;
bool isAccessPointMode = true; // Start in AP mode by
default

// Function to read temperature and humidity
String getSensorData() {
  float temperature = dht.readTemperature();
  float humidity = dht.readHumidity();

  if (isnan(temperature) || isnan(humidity)) {
    return "Failed to read from DHT sensor!";
  }

  String data = "Temperature: " + String(temperature) +
"° C<br>"
                "Humidity: " + String(humidity) + "%";
  return data;
}

// Function to handle requests to root URL
void handleRoot() {
  String html = "<h1>ESP32 IoT Weather Station</h1>"
                "<p>Mode: " + String(isStationMode ?
"Station" : "Access Point") + "</p>"
                "<p>Sensor Data:<br>" + getSensorData() +
"</p>"
                "<p><a href=¥"/sta¥"><button>Switch to
Station Mode</button></a></p>"
                "<p><a href=¥"/ap¥"><button>Switch to Access
Point Mode</button></a></p>"
```

```
                    "<p><a href=¥"/staap¥"><button>Switch to
STA+AP Mode</button></a></p>"
                    "<p><a href=¥"/scan¥"><button>Scan for
Networks</button></a></p>"
                    "<p><a href=¥"/smartconfig¥"><button>Start
Smart Config</button></a></p>";
  server.send(200, "text/html", html);
}

// Function to switch to Station Mode
void handleStationMode() {
  isStationMode = true;
  isAccessPointMode = false;
  WiFi.mode(WIFI_STA);
  WiFi.begin(staSSID, staPassword);
  server.send(200, "text/plain", "Switched to Station
Mode");
}

// Function to switch to Access Point Mode
void handleAccessPointMode() {
  isStationMode = false;
  isAccessPointMode = true;
  WiFi.mode(WIFI_AP);
  WiFi.softAP(apSSID, apPassword);
  server.send(200, "text/plain", "Switched to Access Point
Mode");
}

// Function to switch to STA+AP Mode
void handleStationAccessPointMode() {
  isStationMode = true;
  isAccessPointMode = true;
  WiFi.mode(WIFI_AP_STA);
  WiFi.begin(staSSID, staPassword);
  WiFi.softAP(apSSID, apPassword);
  server.send(200, "text/plain", "Switched to STA+AP Mode");
}
```

```cpp
// Function to scan for available networks
void handleScanNetworks() {
  int n = WiFi.scanNetworks();
  String networks = "<h1>Available Networks</h1>";
  for (int i = 0; i < n; ++i) {
    networks += "<p>" + String(WiFi.SSID(i)) + " (" +
String(WiFi.RSSI(i)) + " dBm)</p>";
  }
  server.send(200, "text/html", networks);
}

// Function to start Smart Config
void handleSmartConfig() {
  WiFi.beginSmartConfig();
  server.send(200, "text/plain", "Started Smart Config.
Please use the ESP-Touch app to configure.");
  while (!WiFi.smartConfigDone()) {
    delay(500);
    Serial.print(".");
  }
  Serial.println("¥nSmart Config completed.");
}

// Function to handle LED ON command
void handleLEDOn() {
  digitalWrite(ledPin, HIGH);
  server.send(200, "text/plain", "LED is ON");
}

// Function to handle LED OFF command
void handleLEDOff() {
  digitalWrite(ledPin, LOW);
  server.send(200, "text/plain", "LED is OFF");
}

void setup() {
  Serial.begin(115200);
pinMode ( ledPin, OUTPUT);
  // Initialize DHT sensor
```

```
dht.begin();

// Set up web server routes
server.on("/", handleRoot);
server.on("/sta", handleStationMode);
server.on("/ap", handleAccessPointMode);
server.on("/staap", handleStationAccessPointMode);
server.on("/scan", handleScanNetworks);
server.on("/smartconfig", handleSmartConfig);

// Start in Access Point Mode by default
WiFi.softAP(apSSID, apPassword);
server.begin();
Serial.println("Web server started");
}

void loop() {
  // Handle incoming client requests
  server.handleClient();
}
```

Save and Run

1. **Open the Arduino IDE** and create a new sketch.
2. **Copy the project code** above into the new sketch.
3. **Connect your ESP32** to your computer via USB.
4. **Configure the Arduino IDE**:
   - Go to **Tools > Board** and select **ESP32 Dev Module**.
   - Go to **Tools > Port** and choose the appropriate COM port.
5. **Upload the code** by clicking on the **Upload button**.

Check Output

1. **Open the Serial Monitor** in the Arduino IDE (Tools > Serial Monitor).
2. **Set the baud rate** to **115200**.

3. **Connect a device to the ESP32's Access Point** with SSID "ESP32_WeatherStation" and password "12345678".
4. **Open a web browser and go to** http://192.168.4.1/.
5. **View the weather data (temperature and humidity)** on the web interface and use the controls to switch modes or scan networks.

ESP32 IoT Weather Station

Mode: Access Point

Sensor Data:
Temperature: 29.70°C
Humidity: 99.90%

Switch to Station Mode

Switch to Access Point Mode

Switch to STA+AP Mode

Scan for Networks

Start Smart Config

Project Summary

This project demonstrates how to use an ESP32 to create a multi-functional **IoT Weather Station** with various network configurations, including:

- **Station Mode** for sending data to the internet.
- **Access Point Mode** for local access to the weather data.
- **STA+AP Mode** for simultaneous local and internet connectivity.
- **Smart Config for easy network configuration.**

- **Web server integration** for a user-friendly interface to display sensor data and control settings.

The **ESP32 IoT Weather Station** provides a flexible and dynamic solution for monitoring environmental conditions, making it ideal for IoT applications where remote monitoring and control are required.

3. Project: ESP32 Home Automation System: Control and Monitor Devices Using Multiple Wi-Fi Modes

Project Overview

This project will guide you through building a comprehensive **ESP32 Home Automation System** that allows for remote monitoring and control of devices (e.g., lights, fans, and sensors) using various networking modes on the ESP32. The system will support:

- **Station Mode (STA)** for connecting to an existing Wi-Fi network and controlling devices over the internet.
- **Access Point Mode (AP)** to create a local network for direct device control.
- **STA+AP Mode** for simultaneous internet and local network control.
- **Wi-Fi Scan** to detect available networks for configuration.
- **Wi-Fi Smart Config** to configure network settings using a smartphone.
- **Web Server** to provide a web-based interface for device control and monitoring.
- **Integration with sensors and relays** to automate tasks.

The goal is to create a smart home solution where the ESP32 can act as the central hub, enabling users to control devices remotely and monitor environmental conditions.

Project Goals

- **Enable remote control of multiple home devices** (e.g., lights, fans) using relays.

- **Provide real-time monitoring of sensor data** (e.g., temperature, humidity, motion detection).
- **Allow for flexible network connectivity using Station, AP, and STA+AP modes**.
- **Host a web server for device control and monitoring**.
- **Easily configure Wi-Fi settings using Smart Config**.
- **Scan and display available networks for easy selection**.
- **Provide a user-friendly web interface for device control and status monitoring**.

Components Required

- **ESP32 development board**
- **Relay modules** (for controlling devices)
- **DHT22 or DHT11 sensor** (for temperature and humidity monitoring)
- **PIR motion sensor** (optional, for motion detection)
- **Resistors (10kΩ)** for DHT sensor
- **Jumper wires and breadboard**
- **Arduino IDE** with ESP32 libraries installed

Circuit Diagram

1. **Relay Module Connections**:
   - **VCC** to **3.3V** on ESP32
   - **GND** to **GND** on ESP32
   - **IN1, IN2, ...** to **GPIO 5, GPIO 18, ...** (depending on how many relays you are using)
2. **DHT Sensor Connections**:
   - **VCC** to **3.3V** on ESP32
   - **GND** to **GND** on ESP32
   - **DATA** to **GPIO 4** on ESP32 (or another GPIO pin)
3. **PIR Motion Sensor Connections** (optional):
   - **VCC** to **3.3V** on ESP32
   - **GND** to **GND** on ESP32
   - **OUT** to **GPIO 12** on ESP32 (or another GPIO pin)
4. **Resistor (10kΩ)** between **VCC and DATA** pin of the DHT sensor.

Project Code

```
#include <WiFi.h>
#include <WebServer.h>
#include <DHT.h>

// Define DHT sensor type and pin
#define DHTTYPE DHT22 // Change to DHT11 if using DHT11
sensor
#define DHTPIN 4       // Pin where the DHT sensor is
connected

DHT dht(DHTPIN, DHTTYPE);

// Web server running on port 80
WebServer server(80);

// Access Point credentials
const char* apSSID = "ESP32_Home_Automation";
const char* apPassword = "12345678";

// Station Mode credentials (default)
const char* staSSID = "Your_SSID";
const char* staPassword = "Your_PASSWORD";

// Relay pins for controlling devices
const int relay1Pin = 5;
const int relay2Pin = 18;

// PIR motion sensor pin
const int pirPin = 12;

// Network mode flags
bool isStationMode = false;
bool isAccessPointMode = true; // Start in AP mode by
default
```

```cpp
// Function to read temperature and humidity
String getSensorData() {
  float temperature = dht.readTemperature();
  float humidity = dht.readHumidity();

  if (isnan(temperature) || isnan(humidity)) {
    return "Failed to read from DHT sensor!";
  }

  String data = "Temperature: " + String(temperature) +
"° C<br>"
                "Humidity: " + String(humidity) + "%";
  return data;
}

// Function to check motion sensor state
String getMotionStatus() {
  int motionDetected = digitalRead(pirPin);
  return motionDetected ? "Motion Detected" : "No Motion";
}

// Function to handle requests to root URL
void handleRoot() {
  String html = "<h1>ESP32 Home Automation System</h1>"
                "<p>Mode: " + String(isStationMode ?
"Station" : "Access Point") + "</p>"
                "<p>Sensor Data:<br>" + getSensorData() +
"</p>"
                "<p>Motion Status: " + getMotionStatus() +
"</p>"
                "<p><a href=¥"/sta¥"><button>Switch to
Station Mode</button></a></p>"
                "<p><a href=¥"/ap¥"><button>Switch to Access
Point Mode</button></a></p>"
                "<p><a href=¥"/staap¥"><button>Switch to
STA+AP Mode</button></a></p>"
                "<p><a href=¥"/scan¥"><button>Scan for
Networks</button></a></p>"
```

```cpp
                   "<p><a href=¥"/smartconfig¥"><button>Start
Smart Config</button></a></p>"
                   "<p><a href=¥"/relay1on¥"><button>Turn Relay
1 ON</button></a></p>"
                   "<p><a href=¥"/relay1off¥"><button>Turn
Relay 1 OFF</button></a></p>"
                   "<p><a href=¥"/relay2on¥"><button>Turn Relay
2 ON</button></a></p>"
                   "<p><a href=¥"/relay2off¥"><button>Turn
Relay 2 OFF</button></a></p>";
  server.send(200, "text/html", html);
}

// Function to switch to Station Mode
void handleStationMode() {
  isStationMode = true;
  isAccessPointMode = false;
  WiFi.mode(WIFI_STA);
  WiFi.begin(staSSID, staPassword);
  server.send(200, "text/plain", "Switched to Station
Mode");
}

// Function to switch to Access Point Mode
void handleAccessPointMode() {
  isStationMode = false;
  isAccessPointMode = true;
  WiFi.mode(WIFI_AP);
  WiFi.softAP(apSSID, apPassword);
  server.send(200, "text/plain", "Switched to Access Point
Mode");
}

// Function to switch to STA+AP Mode
void handleStationAccessPointMode() {
  isStationMode = true;
  isAccessPointMode = true;
  WiFi.mode(WIFI_AP_STA);
  WiFi.begin(staSSID, staPassword);
```

```cpp
  WiFi.softAP(apSSID, apPassword);
  server.send(200, "text/plain", "Switched to STA+AP Mode");
}

// Function to scan for available networks
void handleScanNetworks() {
  int n = WiFi.scanNetworks();
  String networks = "<h1>Available Networks</h1>";
  for (int i = 0; i < n; ++i) {
    networks += "<p>" + String(WiFi.SSID(i)) + " (" +
String(WiFi.RSSI(i)) + " dBm)</p>";
  }
  server.send(200, "text/html", networks);
}

// Function to start Smart Config
void handleSmartConfig() {
  WiFi.beginSmartConfig();
  server.send(200, "text/plain", "Started Smart Config.
Please use the ESP-Touch app to configure.");
  while (!WiFi.smartConfigDone()) {
    delay(500);
    Serial.print(".");
  }
  Serial.println("\nSmart Config completed.");
}

// Functions to control relays
void handleRelay1On() {
  digitalWrite(relay1Pin, LOW); // Relay ON (active low)
  server.send(200, "text/plain", "Relay 1 is ON");
}

void handleRelay1Off() {
  digitalWrite(relay1Pin, HIGH); // Relay OFF (active low)
  server.send(200, "text/plain", "Relay 1 is OFF");
}

void handleRelay2On() {
```

```cpp
  digitalWrite(relay2Pin, LOW); // Relay ON (active low)
  server.send(200, "text/plain", "Relay 2 is ON");
}

void handleRelay2Off() {
  digitalWrite(relay2Pin, HIGH); // Relay OFF (active low)
  server.send(200, "text/plain", "Relay 2 is OFF");
}

void setup() {
  Serial.begin(115200);

  // Initialize DHT sensor
  dht.begin();

  // Initialize relay pins
  pinMode(relay1Pin, OUTPUT);
  pinMode(relay2Pin, OUTPUT);
  digitalWrite(relay1Pin, HIGH); // Set to HIGH (OFF)
initially
  digitalWrite(relay2Pin, HIGH); // Set to HIGH (OFF)
initially

  // Initialize PIR motion sensor
  pinMode(pirPin, INPUT);

  // Set up web server routes
  server.on("/", handleRoot);
  server.on("/sta", handleStationMode);
  server.on("/ap", handleAccessPointMode);
  server.on("/staap", handleStationAccessPointMode);
  server.on("/scan", handleScanNetworks);
  server.on("/smartconfig", handleSmartConfig);
  server.on("/relay1on", handleRelay1On);
  server.on("/relay1off", handleRelay1Off);
  server.on("/relay2on", handleRelay2On);
  server.on("/relay2off", handleRelay2Off);

  // Start in Access Point Mode by default
```

```
  WiFi.softAP(apSSID, apPassword);
  server.begin();
  Serial.println("Web server started");
}

void loop() {
  // Handle incoming client requests
  server.handleClient();
}
```

Save and Run

1. **Open the Arduino IDE** and create a new sketch.
2. **Copy the project code** above into the new sketch.
3. **Connect your ESP32** to your computer via USB.
4. **Configure the Arduino IDE**:
   o Go to **Tools > Board** and select **ESP32 Dev Module**.
   o Go to **Tools > Port** and choose the appropriate COM port.
5. **Upload the code** by clicking on the **Upload button**.

Check Output

1. **Open the Serial Monitor** in the Arduino IDE (Tools > Serial Monitor).
2. **Set the baud rate** to **115200**.
3. **Connect a device to the ESP32's Access Point** with SSID "ESP32_Home_Automation" and password "12345678".
4. **Open a web browser and go to** http://192.168.4.1/.
5. **Use the web interface to control relays, switch modes, scan networks, and monitor sensor data.**

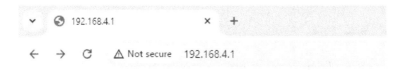

ESP32 Home Automation System

Mode: Access Point

Sensor Data:
Temperature: 28.50Â°C
Humidity: 99.90%

Motion Status: No Motion

Switch to Station Mode

Switch to Access Point Mode

Switch to STA+AP Mode

Scan for Networks

Start Smart Config

Turn Relay 1 ON

Turn Relay 1 OFF

Turn Relay 2 ON

Turn Relay 2 OFF

Project Summary

This project demonstrates how to build a versatile **ESP32 Home Automation System** that can:

- **Control devices using relays**.
- **Monitor environmental conditions with a DHT sensor**.
- **Detect motion using a PIR sensor**.
- **Switch between multiple network modes (Station, AP, STA+AP)**.
- **Host a web server for easy control and monitoring**.

- **Use Smart Config for network setup.**
- **Scan for available networks.**

The **ESP32 Home Automation System** serves as a powerful example of integrating various ESP32 networking capabilities and sensor controls, making it suitable for smart home applications.

ESP32 Smart Energy Meter: Monitor and Control Power Consumption Using Multiple Wi-Fi Modes

Project Overview

This project will guide you through creating a **Smart Energy Meter** using the ESP32, where you can monitor and control power cons